FROME

A SPECIAL TOWN

A BOOK WRITTEN BY PEOPLE
INTERESTED IN FROME'S PAST, PRESENT
AND, IN PARTICULAR, FUTURE

*Produced for the people of Frome by the Rotary Club
of Frome, in celebration of its 70th birthday*

PRINTED BY BUTLER & TANNER
FOR THE PEOPLE OF FROME

Contributing Authors (alphabetical)

Bob Ashford
Bob Beacham
Peter Belham
Tony Brown
Arthur Court
Hilary Daniel
Insp Stephen Gazzard
Derek Gill
Rodney Goodall
Julie Grail
Dr Stephanie Greshon
Derek Harman-Trick
Owen Hillier
Rev Ward Jones
Malcolm Lloyd
Michael McGarvie
John Moxon
Sheila Nicholson
Dennis Pattinson
Andrew Prince
Alan Sandall
Leslie White
Malcolm Williams

Winners of Under 19 Essays:
1 Chris Eales   2 Leeandra Curtain-Marten   3 Ken Vernon
Winners of Under 13 Essays:
1 Jessie Taylor   2 Anna Simms   3 Andrew Pattison

Photographers from Frome Photographic Society

David Bathard
Peter Bruton
Roger Miles
David Moon
Pip Rabbitts
Gerry Russell
Greg Wright
and many other photographers, past and present

Editor: Rotarian Dr John Moxon, MBE
Consultant Editor: Rotarian Alan Sandall
Published by: Rotary Club of Frome ©
Graphic Design: Design/Section
Colour Reproduction: Radstock Repro, Midsomer Norton
Printed and Bound by: Butler & Tanner Group of Companies
Paper from: Stora, Sweden and Precision Papers, Yeovil

ISBN: 0 9526836 0 1.

CONTENTS

FOREWORD

Restored Rook Lane Chapel of 1606 heads the attractive cottages in Bath Street.

The small emblem of the Rotary movement on the front cover is recognised across the world. I will say no more about Rotary because this book is about Frome, this ancient and proud market town, and its people.

The purpose of the book is to tell the world, in a kaleidoscope of words and pictures, the many good things about this Somerset town. Many of its people responded, without hesitation, to make this book possible. Butler & Tanner saw immediately the possible benefits to the town and offered its talented services without charge. The quality of their production speaks for itself.

Some of Frome's special atmosphere is one that is often found in towns with an ancient heritage, 1,300 years, in our case. Many visitors come, and some stay on, because the past has not been bulldozed away with the abandonment found in so many other towns. The modern estates developed harmoniously on the edges of the town have given good-life opportunities to the many who have settled there and become involved in the hive of activities going on in the town.

We are proud of our widely-known industries, some in the front-line of methods and technology, yet still bearing family names. Others have set up here to benefit from a place where happy skilled staff make a better work force. We too, have had our unemployment problems, but these have reduced sharply.

I hope this book will tell the true story of Frome. Some large employers might note that Frome is near enough to national trunk roads for a huge fleet of large quarry lorries, and J.R. Harding's massive transports' daily journeys, without its inhabitants being polluted by the constant roaring road-sound of nearby motorways. If that encourages them to fill a space in our new trading estates, we would be delighted.

My thanks to everyone who made this book possible.

⌐ Alan Sandall ⌐
President of the Rotary Club of Frome

PREFACE

I was delighted when I heard about plans to produce a book celebrating Frome and the anniversary of the Rotary Club. I would like to extend my heartfelt thanks to the Rotary Club, and the many other individuals and organisations in the town who have made the production possible. It is this same spirit of co-operation and partnership that will enable Frome to prosper into the 21st century.

Frome is a town of remarkable contrasts, and its beauty, which constantly turns visitors into residents, lies in its historical buildings, its community facilities and the warmth and creativity of its people.

Frome already has an abundance of resources which makes it the envy of neighbouring towns; its excellent schools, community education and youth clubs; its arts and performing arts organisations, the Merlin Theatre, the Memorial Hall, Ecos and the Black Swan Guild; the new Library and Tourist Information building, the Leisure Centre and thriving sports clubs.

Despite the current economic recession and the loss of many jobs in recent years in Frome's traditional manufacturing industries the town still has many successful companies with international reputations which have made Frome their home.

At the same time the town retains a distinctly rural feel, and with some of the most beautiful areas in Britain on our doorstep it is not surprising that increasing numbers of people are coming as tourists.

Frome is also on the verge of many exciting projects. The riverside enhancement scheme and the recognition by the National Rivers Authority that the river which runs through our town could and should be the centrepiece of Frome. The old Cheese and Grain building shortly to pass to the Town Council as a new Market and community facility. The plans for a new Town Museum. The creation of an artificial playing surface and expansion of the Leisure Centre. Plans for town centre management and enhancement and a new town centre development, long awaited and nearing initial agreement. The refurbishment of Rook Lane Chapel. The regeneration of Catherine Hill. Social housing developments in The Piggeries and the demolition and rebuilding of council housing in the Trinity area. The list is endless and again reflects the wealth of energy and ideas alive in the town.

It is this energy and creativity that has created present day Frome and I believe will ensure its growing success. Along with the new Town Council I share a vision of a Frome that looks to the future but does not ignore its past and which meets the needs of and encourages all its citizens to prosper together.

Cllr Bob Ashford
Mayor of Frome

ACKNOWLEDGEMENTS

The Rotary Club of Frome wish to thank the following,
without whose help this book would not have been possible:

All contributors who wrote the articles

The Frome Photographic Society and all the other photographers

All who generously lent photographs

Glyn Martin, whose beautiful painting of Cheap Street is on the cover.

Scenic Maps Ltd, of Bridstow who let us use their splendid map,
larger versions of which delight Frome shoppers.

Butler & Tanner, whose skilled printing is for all to see.

Their staff and those at their brilliant design company
have been most patient and understanding.

Stora of Sweden, and Precision Papers, Yeovil for so
generously supplying the quality paper.

The many who supplied information used in the articles.

Those with ideas and suggestions.

The editor and his team.

Those who had faith that the idea would bear fruit.

INTRODUCTION

Samuel Cuzner in 1866 claimed to produce the first book on Froome-Selwood, and drew on his multi talents as a stationer, perfumer, hairdresser (using a patent rotary hair brushing machine!), stockist of cutlery, china and glass of vertu, French lamp oil, fish and dessert papers, his own hair restorer, lime juice and brilliantine. All these, he freely advertised amongst others, throughout his excellent book. Who was the printer? Messrs Butler & Tanner.

My connections with the word 'rotary', is not from patent hair brushing machines, but with the Rotary Movement, its name derives from originally meeting in members' houses in rotation. My only claim to a 'first' is that I believe that this is the first cased book on Frome from multiple authors. All modern authors and historians who have written their own excellent books on Frome have contributed to this book, and I am profoundly grateful to them.

Unlike Mr Cuzner's, there is no advertising in this book, due to the generosity of all authors and photographers giving their services free. Frome's famous international printers Messrs Butler & Tanner have offered most generously to print and produce to high quality this book as a contribution to the Town from whom they draw their skilled workforce.

When the current President of the Rotary Club of Frome suggested the Club should produce a book of Frome for the town, to celebrate our 70th birthday, I was delighted to accept the challenge, and the modest beginnings of his idea have somehow grown more ambitious as the book took shape. I and my Club are deeply grateful to all who have most generously contributed. As inexperienced as Samuel Cuzner, being a retired general medical practitioner, I join him in quoting Izaak Walton, "I am but a gatherer and disposer of other men's stuff."

— John Moxon —
Editor

Town map of Frome. Acknowledgement Scenic Maps Ltd.

Murrhardt

Château-Gontier

CHAPTER I

FROM THE PAST TO
THE FUTURE

— Derek Gill —

About 685AD a group of monks led by the Abbot of Malmesbury, St. Aldhelm, found their way to a clearing on a small plateau in the great Selwood Forest on the hillside above the river. Here they cleared the ground and built a small stone church which they dedicated to St. John the Baptist. This was a time of uncertainty to which the small group of monks brought the conviction of their faith to the scattered people living in the area.

So Frome was founded and began to grow. It gradually became the centre for agriculture with a market, so much so that by the Domesday survey of 1086 it had three mills paying 25s- and a market which yielded 46s8d a year. The surrounding forests provided hunting for the king who held the manor. The Somerset County Museum recently acquired a coin minted in Frome.

As the Middle Ages progressed so another industry developed which was to make Frome a much more important and prosperous town. With so many sheep rearing areas around – the Mendips, Salisbury Plain and even the Cotswolds – and with its river, it was not surprising that Frome became the centre for cloth making to rival Bradford and Trowbridge.

The industry reached its peak in the 16th to 18th centuries and resulted in an expansion of the population, the town acting as a magnet. So we have a wealth of buildings of that period which fortunately have survived, making Frome an architectural gem which is now recognised nationally. The Trinity area, as it is now called, was developed from 1660 to 1720 to provide homes for the artisans.

Field names proved a clue to this industry. So behind Willow Vale was Rack Close, where the dyed cloth was spread out to dry. Goulds Ground was Cut hedges, where the hedges were kept low so the wind would not be hindered from drying the cloth.

Before 1856 natural dyes were used so the Trinity area was developed on the oadground, or wode ground, a reminder of the plant that made a blue dye. Yew dyed cloth brown, lichen, which needed chlorine from urine to break it down, purple, and hedge bedstraw dyed it red.

In 1713, whilst Trowbridge had 4 clothiers and Bradford 25, Frome had 54, plus a further 33 in neighbouring villages. In 1745 'seven waggons have been sent out for cloth weekly for Blackwell Hall (in London) and each of the waggons have been known to hold 140 pieces'.

The last period of prosperity was during the Napoleonic wars when Frome produced blue cloth for army uniforms. As the 19th century progressed so the industry declined, due largely to competition from Lancashire and the North of England.

Frome was in a bad way with increasing unemployment. In 1823 twelve Frome clothiers went bankrupt and the Poor Rate increased alarmingly. Sheppards Mill at Spring Gardens, the largest employer, closed in 1878, although Tuckers continued at Wallbridge until 1965.

What was needed was regeneration. Already Cockeys, who first cast church bells here about 1685, had changed to cast iron and engineering for the blossoming gas industry. It is not surprising that the town had gas street lighting as early as 1832. In the 1850s two enterprising entrepreneurs developed other industries, almost by accident.

John Webb Singer, a watchmaker in the Market Place, using an interest in metal, made a pair of brass candlesticks for a local vicar and accidentally hit a ready market. This was a time of re-awakened interest in liturgy in the Church of England, by the Tractarians. Their ideas were brought to Frome by the appointment of Vicar Bennett to St. John's in 1852.

Singer's watchmaking took second place to his art metal work and the firm was born. The firm became internationally renowned for the skill of its work, the native talent of its employees and the artistic skill of the Singer family.

In the 1880s a meeting with three leading London sculptors persuaded Singer to build a foundry to cast statues too. So for 40 years the firm cast statues of high quality including Boadicea on the Embankment, Justice on the Old Bailey, King Alfred at Winchester, and the lions for the Rhodes memorial at Capetown.

Concurrently, a chance purchase of a small printing press by William Langford, a chemist on Bath Street, to print labels for his medicine bottle, led to the development of Butler and Tanner, now another major local industry. This firm expanded in the Trinity area where its first factory building still exists.

Today Frome is at a crossroads. The decline in its industrial base of recent years could continue, but there is the potential for that not to happen. The skills of its work people could help regenerate it and be an asset to Frome. History can repeat itself, for a temporary decline can be reversed by imagination and foresight, to bring growth and prosperity again.

The seeds of this growth are already apparent. The investment possibilty of the Singer's factory on a new site is one recognition of the engineering skills of the employees. The development of wood preservatives by the expansion of Cuprinol is another; whilst the cattle market outgrew its town centre site, and is now thriving on the edge of town. All this shows faith in the potential for regeneration.

Busy Cheap Street's fast flowing stream is a magnet to children, who chase matchstick boats and jump till they miss.

The potential in Frome was recently recognised in a survey by the Civic Trust, a national body. Its author had not visited Frome before conducting his survey, so he cannot be said to be biased, but he quickly recognised the advantages of Frome.

Frome has to stand up for itself again, as it has in the past, and to sell itself as a town of skilled work people set in beautiful surroundings. If Mr. Singer could develop his art metal work 150 miles from London, so can Frome again develop new industries. The phoenix on one of Frome's buildings is surely a good omen.

CHAPTER 2

LIVING HERE

— Hilary Daniel —

During the fifty years that have elapsed since the end of World War Two, well within the adult lifespan of many of its townspeople, Frome has been completely transformed.

Its population has doubled, its built-up area has expanded threefold, and its communications have improved out of all recognition. Frome's social and recreational facilities have been greatly enhanced, and its industries and commerce, the means by which it earns its living, have been revolutionised.

The additional inhabitants have come in mostly from far afield. Many of the new houses that have been built since the war were destined to attract either young families, or older people on the verge of retirement, and they have brought in people with wide ranges of skills and experience. A significant proportion of the newcomers has consisted of employees

Tranquillity at Great Elm, sight of Jackdaws Studio and the Music Festival.

Bishop Ken is buried in this churchyard, past which winds Frome's ancient Gentle Street.

of businesses or Government offices in Bath or Bristol, who have found the 30 or 40 minutes' journey to work a small price to pay for the advantage of living in a smaller and more caring community, while among the older group there is scarcely an organisation in the town which has not come to rely on the skills and experience of new Frome residents in the running of its affairs.

Not only has there been a proliferation of new housing sites, but most of Frome's important range of 17th century industrial housing was saved from wholesale demolition during the 1960s, and has now been carefully restored to provide a wide range of historic homes close to the town centre.

Unfortunately there was a long period during which Frome's industry and commerce were unable to offer too wide a range of employment opportunities. Having been one of the earliest towns in the West Country to have benefited from the Industrial Revolution – Cobbett called it "a little Manchester" when he rode through during the 1820s – the end of the war found it with a significant number of its factories still located on restricted sites in the central area of the town, where opportunities for re-equipment and expansion were limited. As a result, when in subsequent years parent companies decided on renewal, several of them re-located elsewhere, leaving their Frome branches to continue only on a limited scale, or even to close down entirely.

Accordingly, Frome became an unemployment black-spot during the 1980s, and enormous efforts have had to be made by Local Government and others to reverse this unhappy trend. It is good to be able to report that the town has now begun a slow climb up through the statistics, and its unemployment rate is now well in line with regional averages. The Marston Trading Estate is lined with modern factories and depots, and wide areas on the town's outskirts have been set aside for future commercial development as the country comes out of recession.

Although industrial employment was sagging, Frome greatly expanded its professional and office base during the 1980s. All four major banks are flourishing in the town, and the numbers of professionals such as doctors, solicitors, financial

Balloons over Longleat.

consultants, surveyors and the like have significantly increased. On the agricultural side, instead of losing its weekly market as so many old market towns have done, Frome has found a new out-of-town site, and the excellent facilities provided there have transformed Frome Market into one of the most active and rapidly expanding in the whole West Country, accompanied by a host of supportive services such as legal, financial and equipment sales. The annual Frome Show in September is also one of the most important one-day agricultural shows for miles around.

Strong and informed local opposition during the 1970s and 1980s to hasty schemes for new shopping prevented Frome from having its heart torn out to make way for unthinking

standardised re-development. While would-be developers at the time warned that this opposition would lead to Frome being left far behind in the commercial race, the result has in fact been quite the opposite. Not only has the town escaped the faceless and tasteless rows of shops forced upon so many other communities in the mad rush for development a decade ago, but the delay has resulted in a vast former industrial site adjoining the main shopping centre becoming available. There is now every prospect that the re-development when it comes will be a well-thought-out and sympathetic one, ready to launch the town into the 21st century, rather than the unimaginative and standardised concrete boxes that would have been put up if Frome had allowed itself to be swept up in the property boom-or-bust of 1988.

Another excellent and progressive step has been the involvement of the whole community in the planning process by the setting up of the Frome Task Force, a committee embracing all branches of local government and many other local interests, both public and private, which thoroughly investigates and weighs up policy proposals before they become too hard-set to allow for sensible modification in the light of experience. This is a local initiative which is likely to provide an inspiration to communities all over the country.

Leisure and sporting interest are well catered for; not only are there dedicated grounds and buildings for the main team sports of Cricket and both Association and Rugby Football, but there is a Sports Centre with a large swimming pool and many other facilities. There are two theatres, and an open-air amphitheatre, and Frome has retained, and even rebuilt, a cinema, when so many much larger towns have lost theirs. There are Societies in the town for every imaginable branch of arts and crafts, and special efforts are made during school holidays to provide varied programmes of activities for children.

Frome has a fortunate position within easy reach of both Bristol Channel and English Channel resorts, and a large sector of the country, from Eastern Cornwall to Brighton, London, Birmingham and Central Wales, can be visited comfortably within a day's drive. Frome has its own station, and there are express rail connections in all directions from nearby Westbury. Motorways or improved A roads to all parts of the country can readily be reached, and there is no built-up area between Frome and London on the A362–A36–A303–M3s route.

The sleepy backwater of 1945 has become a place with a great potential as a touring centre, as well as retaining its primary function of being a very pleasant town in which to live and work.

CHAPTER 3

WHAT'S SO SPECIAL ABOUT LIVING IN FROME?

— Peter Belham —

Why Frome? Why live in Frome/shop in Frome/locate your business in Frome/come to Frome for your entertainment? Why not Stroud, or Barnstaple, or Ilkley or Wokingham?

What is so special about living or working in Frome? Why is it that in these days when ease of communications means than many of us can within reason live and work almost anywhere in this country, a considerable number of us wish to come here and stay here?

One answer must surely be the surroundings of the town - the pleasant countryside and the easy access to Bath, Bristol, Longleat, Wells and a great number of delightful villages.

But it isn't just that. If the town itself was without a distinctive character of its own, without interest or charm, the nature of its surroundings alone would not attract people to it.

Fortunately, in spite of the pressures which are operating throughout the country with the apparent intention of making every town like every other, our town still had its distinctive features.

It has more listed buildings than any other town in Somerset, it has retained in its central area its medieval street pattern. Its steep hills, while a trial to ageing citizens and a cause of slow-moving traffic, enables us to have all sorts of glimpses of half-hidden views. Its roof-scapes in particular I find very attractive.

But however attractive or important its physical attributes, a town depends more on its people and on the activities which go on within it for its character. I have lived in Frome while its population has more than doubled from the 11,000 which it had when the Second World War ended; and of course the sheer size of the town has also grown as more and more roads and houses have pushed out into the surrounding countryside. Yet, in some important respects it has retained the features which I recognised when we first came here to live.

In particular I think of the friendliness and the sheer generosity of the people. We have always regarded self-help as important and over the years we have responded to many appeals for the provision of facilities which we could not rely on outside authorities to provide, and the response has always been very generous.

Frome has also retained its tradition of self-help in its social life and particularly in the provision of entertainment. The shows of the Operatic Society are the most obvious though not the only example. And if you look at the local Residents' Handbook, you will find that there are over 100 voluntary organisations, catering one would think for every possible interest, operating in the town.

So: a lot of the pleasure of living in Frome comes from the friendliness of the people, the surroundings and the sense of history which is inseparable from a place which was first settled more than 1300 years ago, but we have to be careful not to be so wrapped up in our past that we become more like a museum than a living community.

A town also needs to be forward-looking and to have the kind of vibrant, pulsating life that comes from having confidence in the future. Two severe recessions in the last 15 years have done something to dent that confidence and it is easy enough to see signs of decay and to be impatient for the apparently interminable discussions about plans to be replaced by positive action.

But we do have growth points and these give us encouragement for the future. Our town contains firms which have an international reputation, firms of which any town might be proud. A walk round our industrial estates shows that we have a great variety of businesses which have a growth potential; and we have the possibility of further growth because we have available other sites, which can attract new firms into the town.

Perhaps most encouraging of all is the great success of the Frome Market near the edge of town, at Standerwick. Not only has this rapidly achieved a considerable reputation throughout the south of England, but it also represents in itself a kind of parable, a lesson for the future.

Having been in danger of decay because of the disadvantages of an outdated site in the town centre, it has risen like a phoenix in the new surroundings. It shows what can be achieved through courage and initiative and it provides an example that can be copied in other parts of our economy and our community life.

So: we have in Frome the solid foundation of a long history, the benefits of a pleasant way of life in the present, and signs of hope for the future – reasons enough for believing that there is something special about living in Frome.

Peter, much loved by all who knew him, died suddenly after an operation, shortly after writing this article. We think this is a fitting memorial for one who did so much for the town.

CHAPTER 4

THE MERLIN THEATRE
STORY

— *Owen Hillier* —

Just as Martin Luther King had his 'dream' so Frome College Principal, John Fisher, had an inspirational 'dream' that Frome should have its own theatre, built on the College campus. It would be used by the College for teaching drama in school working hours, and at all other times, by the people of Frome as a Community Theatre and Arts Centre. He spoke of this 'dream' in an address to a PTA Meeting in 1969/70, and such was his enthusiasm and intensity of purpose, that he inspired those inexhaustible fund-raisers for the school, to renew their efforts and start raising money for the new theatre!

Somerset County Council made a ten year loan at a favourable interest rate, grants were obtained from South West Arts, various local industries and, especially, the Glubenkian Foundation. This was the time of great upheaval for Frome's schools: the Grammar School became Frome College by taking in the two top forms from the two Secondary Modern Schools, which became Middle Schools.

Messrs Holdaway & Son was erecting the new classrooms, and it was fortunate that such a builder was on site, together with all the necessary equipment. It was able to carry out the two contracts simultaneously. The combined post of Theatre Director and Head of Drama was created and it worked very well, but later became too onerous for one person, so the positions were separated.

After a lot of discussion the name 'Merlin' for the theatre was agreed. It conveyed the idea of the magic and mystery we hoped it would bring. Actor Frank Finlay performed the official opening, and has been followed by hosts of artistes, some of them, eminent. They include David Kossoff, Ian Mackellen and the Royal Shakespeare Company, Brian Blessed, John Lill, Chura Shukasky, the Bournemouth Symphonietta, Gerry and the Pacemakers, George Melly, Chris Barber, Pam Ayres and many others.

The Merlin is renowned for its modern shape, its comfortable bright salmon seats, and unusually roomy knee space. In its wide variety of programmes of classical and pop music, dance, mime, drama, band concerts, amateur productions, one act play competitions, and so on, its brilliant drama and circus workshops for children in the school holidays, are the ones always sold out.

The Director, Administrator, Technician and, later, part-time Marketing Officer, could not run the Theatre without the valuable help of its devoted volunteers. Teams of 'front of house', box office, refreshments, behind stage and other volunteers have built up such a reputation that they are used as an example in other places, of how to run a theatre.

In common with many other such organisations, to tighten the management to cope with modern conditions, the theatre became a limited company, two years ago. A Board of Management, replacing the theatre's Council and Management Committee, which had made the theatre work so successfully for so many years.

Ticket sales pay for most of the artistes' fees, (and if the theatre was as full as in pre-recession times it would pay for all of them), but the theatre relies heavily on grants from South West Arts and Somerset County Council to help pay for staff, heat, light and cleaning, insurance, rates and many other overheads. Frome and Mendip District Council also help, as do fund-raising efforts.

What of the future? Frome without its Merlin Theatre would be unthinkable. Its full programme of events, its art gallery, the friendly staff and volunteers, all make it a pleasure to attend. The Memorial Hall fulfils quite different needs, and is not considered a rival; many volunteers work for both of them. A town the size of Frome needs them both. When funds allow, the Merlin has plans to enlarge the foyer and refreshment area and increase the seating, as well as technical and behind stage improvements.

Students rehersing in the Merlin Theatre.

We are confident that the success story of 'The Merlin' will continue, and it will go on to serve the needs of Frome as they grow with its increasing prosperity.

CHAPTER 5

VISITORS' GUIDE

— Rodney Goodall —

Frome's history goes back to c 685 AD, when Aldhelm (Bishop of both Malmesbury and Sherborne, and later canonised as a Saint) founded the Monastery of St John near the River Frome. The name is Anglo-Saxon for a river – the town has never had a 'proper' name. It lay in a clearing in Selwood Forest (of which parts of Longleat are the remnants). The main Parish church of St John stands on or near that site, and being at the heart of the town it is a good place to start a short tour.

Frome cannot be explored by car – all the best parts are in pedestrian streets, but old Frome was remarkably compact, (something like 80% of today's Frome is post 1950). Walk through the church forecourt (cleared in c 1815 to enhance the town's new South approach – Bath Street – into Frome).

Bath Street leads away from Bath – it is named after the then Lord Bath who gave the land for its construction – and was part of a Regency reshaping of the town centre in a late Georgian style. It was specially landscaped: the cedar of Lebanon opposite was planted in 1815, and the ornamental boundary walls built at that time survive in part.

At the bottom of Bath Street is the Market Place, originally divided into the upper and lower markets: the Frome Market was well established by 1086 and is described in the Domesday Survey. (The Cattle Market was relocated to a farm site at Standerwick, about 3 miles away, in 1990, and is one of the largest and most up-to-date in Southern England).

Most of the buildings here in the Market Place are of the 19th century, but the four hostelries are older. The George is Mediaeval (i.e. St George, not the Hanoverian Kings), and the Angel (at the bottom of King Street) is probably pre-1530 because of its name; both the Crown and the Blue Boar date from the end of the 17th century. Frome is rich in its pubs: a map of 1774 shows 43 of them, of which over half are still identifiable, and currently 16 are still trading, although one has been rebuilt.

A small selection of market stalls still trades here on Wednesdays and Saturdays. The road leading out of the Market Place to the north is North Parade, built in 1797 – except for the Frome Literary and Scientific Institute, the Italianate building on the sharp corner site, which is of 1859: the Town Bridge leading to it is a fourth rebuild, of 1821, and apart from one in

Frome Town Bridge, one of only two in the country bearing multi-storey buildings.

Lincoln is the only English bridge still to have multi-storey buildings on it.

Just before the bridge, on the right, is the Blue House of 1721 – originally a boys' grammar school combined with an old ladies' home, it now is a charitable foundation housing old persons of both sexes.

Starting from the Boyle Cross in the Market Place is Cheap Street (literally the Street of the Chapmen, or Merchants) – Frome's first shopping street, and not surprisingly linking the Market Place with the Church. Several houses here are of half-timbered construction, although this is not always obvious.

Go to the top, and up the steps into the church forecourt again. Turn left for a quick detour to see the old blind house – a subterranean chamber in the corner of the churchyard, and for Vicarage Street, which has several old houses including a fine vicarage of 1744 and later.

Go on up the hill. Gentle Street, named after a one-time resident, as are several of Frome's streets and note several fine houses – Argyll House on the right, is of 1768, and several on the left are of late mediaeval date although sometimes later 'Georgianised'.

At the top of this street turn right to the crossroads, noting the fine former Congregational Church of 1707 at the top of Bath Street (the 'least fair' of three fine

Nunney Castle, What are the green areas below the tops of the towers? Answer opposite.

churches built in Frome at the start of the 18th century — the others have gone).

Cross straight over and walk along Christchurch Street West earlier known as 'Top-o-Town' or 'Behind Town'. This represents the 18th century 'Frome Bypass' which enabled traffic for Southampton and London (via Stonehenge) to avoid the steep hills into and out of the town. Note the Pack Horse Inn (c 1730) and the Ship Inn (probably pre 1600), and opposite, West Lodge, a fine house of 1780. Christ Church dates from 1817, with later extensions.

Continue past the shops until you reach Selwood Road, and turn right. You are now in part of the 'New Town' which was built from the prosperity of the woollen industry (Frome's staple until the mid 19th century) between 1675 and 1725 as one of the earliest (if not actually the first) leasehold development. It has recently had its third cycle of restoration (the leases were usually for 99 years) and the Royal Commission for Historic Monuments has published a book about this small area. In the 1960s the whole area was condemned, and about half was demolished to be replaced by very undistinguished council houses (avert your eyes!).

Turn right around the corner of the old printing factory (Butler & Tanner, now Europe's largest privately owned printing press, which started here, is still in Frome, but on a new site). Go left by the Lamb and Fountain (a late 17th century pub) and turn right at the bottom of the hill up to Catherine Street, and turn left here. Notice the variety of old houses as you return either to the church (on the high pavement) or to the Market Place, down Stony Street.

In this perambulation, never more that 200-300 yards from the Market Place, you have seen most of old Frome, which by 1821 had a population of some 11,000 – one of the most concentrated areas of habitation in the country, and almost unique in the South-West of England.

As the woollen industry (which here relied on water power) gradually collapsed many people emigrated as they were thrown out of work, and it was not until 1961 that Frome's population was again about 11,000.

However, the sites of many old mills have been taken over by other industries (dairying, plastics, printing, paints and preservatives) and other industries have developed new sites. Now in part a dormitory town for Bath and Bristol, Frome has nearly 25,000 inhabitants today – which demonstrates the tremendous growth that has occurred since 1960 – and the tremendous amount of green field land swallowed up! Natural boundaries around the town are likely to restrict further growth in most directions, however – perhaps that is just as well!

Answer to question on adjacent page: turn it upside down and look in the moat!

CHAPTER 6

OUR

ENVIRONMENT MATTERS

— Dr Stephanie Greshon —

The importance of preserving and improving the already damaged environment
around us is no longer just the message voiced by seemingly extreme groups.
Damage to the precious ozone layer is seriously and widely recognised, the effects
acid rain are plain to see and the reduced quality of the air we breathe is causing anxiety to
many and physical distress to a growing number. The deterioration in the cleanliness of
our rivers due to industrial and agricultural pollution has been widely recognised and is
being actively addressed.

At the Rio Earth Summit in 1992, 150 countries signed a global action plan called
Agenda 21. This sets out objectives – economic, social and environmental, needing
sustained measures and campaigning to protect the environment into the 21st century.
The participation of local authorities is essential for its success.

The Local Agenda 21 programme for Mendip has been developed through a process of
information gathering about the district's natural resources, people and human activities
which affect the environment. The process led to the publication of the Mendip Environment
Report, in November 1994, designed to help local people care for their own area.

These exciting initiatives, facilitated by Mendip District Council, have resulted in the
development of aims, objectives and action points in a Local Agenda 21 Plan, which have
been developed further through workshops and discussions held throughout the district.

Developing sustainability at the local level requires a long term approach, involving
changes of attitude and individual lifestyles. Mendip's Local Agenda 21 programme is,
therefore, seen as the first step in a long process which will continue into the 21st century.
The Mendip District Plan also emphasises the importance of sustainable development and
provides the underlying framework for a healthy and viable rural economy. It does not mean
that economic growth will be less but that any decisions about new development take into
account the impact on the environment and prevent major adverse impacts from occurring.

In a recent press report, the Mendip district has been described as an environmental
jewel. Living and working within the area, we have a responsibility to protect and enhance
our rich environmental resources, from ancient woodlands, to limestone grasslands and

wetlands. This has been highlighted by the publication of the Mendip Biodiversity Action Plan, the first biodiversity study undertaken by a local authority in the UK.

The great significance of input by small business can be appreciated as the majority of firms in Mendip are small with 91.8% employing 25 persons or less. The Frome business community has been particularly active in supporting local authority environmental initiatives and has been the test bed for several Local Agenda 21 projects. One such initiative has been the Frome River Project which aims to enhance and protect the immediate environment of the River Frome. Several local firms have supported this project, either financially or by providing staff, resources and plants. The stretch of the river which flows though Frome is now an asset which the people of Frome can be proud of.

Annual Raft Race on River Frome.

Other Frome businesses have been quietly turning areas of their grounds into wildlife havens. The staff of Mendip Foods, for example, can enjoy watching wildlife from their office windows, a direct result of sensitive ground management regimes which have regard for the natural environment and the vision of management to seize the opportunities of sustainable development.

For the youth of Frome, schools, Brownie groups and other community associations are involved in the Wildcheck project, where children identify 20 easily recognisable plants and animals in their area. These are surveyed each year and help monitor the district's wildlife resources, providing a valuable record of the continuing quality of the natural environment.

Local Agenda 21 is not just about protecting wildlife but has given rise to economic opportunities. Local businesses are actively seeking to improve their environmental performance by cutting down on waste materials, saving energy, reducing water consumption and recycling wherever possible. By improving energy efficiency, businesses are making a contribution to reducing the greenhouse effect.

As well as helping to protect the environment, these initiatives are allowing firms to exploit opportunities and to avoid threats in a changing market place. Also they are saving money! This is being facilitated by the formation of a Business and the Environment Club, whereby Frome businesses can meet regularly with other Mendip firms in tackling specific environmental issues.

From a social perspective, an innovative project called Age to Age has brought together young and old people in Frome, in story-telling workshops and other activities, where youngsters can learn from their elders about the environment in earlier years. The surprises are that much of our current wisdom is not new thinking at all but is often part of a traditional, sustainable way of life that has become lost over the decades. By working together, both young and old are looking to the future, to see how our quality of life can be sustained without causing detriment to the environment.

From the point of view of Frome's future Local Agenda 21 is good news. It has given rise to opportunities for sustainable economic growth, business opportunities and community projects whereby the people of Frome can work together to protect the Mendip environment and allow it to remain a good and healthy place to live and work in the future.

CHAPTER 7

FROME'S INTERESTING
OLD STREETS

— Michael McGarvie —

hen St. Aldhelm crossed the River Frome on his way from Malmesbury to his Dorset estates, he used a ford on the west side of the present Town Bridge. A path led across the wooded plain, site of the present market place, and meandered up the steep hillside to Keyford, probably a British settlement which existed before Frome was founded.

The path joined a trackway which came from the east and passed into the north-west. Later this track was called Behind Town and, until the expansion of Frome in the late 19th century, lived up to its name.

The eastern end was known as Portway, a name given to routes which linked market towns (from the Latin portus, used for towns as well as ports). Here started also the Ridgeway, still brought to mind by the name of a hamlet, and a network of trackways used by our forebears who were traders and herders of cattle.

Aldhelm was struck by the site of the future Frome and about the year 685 founded a monastery and church there on a bleak, north-facing hillside. Viewing this wild spot, he dedicated it to St. John the Baptist who cried in the wilderness. The wealthy abbot, a relation of King Ine of Wessex, endowed his church richly. Anglo-Saxon kings visited it, humbler folk sought work and safety in its shade.

A settlement grew up which came to be called Frome after the river on which it stood, the name derived from Celtic ffraw, meaning fine, fair or brisk. A market was established which was flourishing by 1086 and is still very much with us. A Witan, or Great Council of the Realm was held in the town; King Edred died here.

In the shadow of these events, the town grew; wattle and daub houses arose along the ancient trackways, later transformed into buildings of half-timber or stone. In-filling created streets which eventually acquired names and, despite the expansion of Frome in recent years, this pattern created in the early Middle Ages survives and is largely intact.

Amongst the most ancient of these is Bridge Street, probably the route used by St. Aldhelm, and named after the five arched bridge which John Leland, the king's antiquary, saw about 1540, and the main entry into Frome from the north from the earliest times until North Parade was cut in 1797.

Ancient Catherine Hill.

In 1810, North Parade was completed by the building of Bath Street, named in honour of the Marquess of Bath, so making a wide thoroughfare through the town to the great benefit of travellers if to the detriment of the picturesque. Nevertheless, the pattern of narrow and irregular streets was not fundamentally disturbed.

The development of Frome is much easier to understand if we conclude that the original market place was below Church Steps where the spring waters, now contained by a Victorian fountain, gushed out to provide Frome with its water supply. The town grew around this market place; below it towards the river, above it towards Keyford in its first stages, then probably east to take in the Vicarage and Rectory and west up Catherine Hill.

The earliest mention of street-names are close to St. John's Church; Church Steps (Scaleram cimiterii) about 1300, Hunger Lane (from old English hangra, land on a steep slope) about the same date, Vicarage Street and 'Cokkestret', now Eagle Lane, both in 1392. Cox Street, perhaps named after Walter le Cok, a Frome taxpayer in 1327, was known as Back Lane and Eagle Lane as well as Cox Street, all at the same time; the Eagle was a pub.

Cheap Street, and Twattle Alley which used to run across the south boundary of the churchyard, fall into the same pattern being derived from Saxon words, ceping, a market, and tot, a lookout place. Cheap Street is mentioned in 1500 (spelled 'chip') when details are extant of a house to be built there. Apple Alley behind Cheap Street and, with its narrow confines, rough paving, and tall, overhanging backsides, a surviving piece of old Frome was also known more prosaicly as Back Lane and Leg of Mutton Lane, a reference to the shape of the block.

King Street is part of mediaeval Frome, although named to mark the Golden Jubilee of George III in 1809. Before that it was either called Back Lane, or, more elegantly, Angel Lane after the pub which may have its origins in the Middle Ages.

Horse and wheeled traffic could not, of course, use the Church Steps. If going east they went up Vicarage Street; to the south and west their route lay by Stony Street, first mentioned in 1568 (but much older) where the road ran on the natural forest marble surface of the hillside.

This led to a dividing of the ways. Catherine Street, formerly St. Catherine and named after a saint whose free chapel lay in the vicinity, led steeply west, merging with Catherine Hill. This was once called Badcox Lane, probably an old field name from Old English cocc, a heap, implying a muck heap. The name still survives for the road junction at the top; an 18th century attempt to call it Seven Dials was shipwrecked on the rock of Frome conservatism.

Returning to our division at the top of Stony Street, the main road went up Palmer Street, so named after a prominent local family about 1750, but in 1571 called John Acot Street after the a' Court family of Frome and Rodden. Here another choice awaited. Rook Lane ran parallel to the present Bath Street in a south-westerly direction coming out on Behind Town at Rook Lane House. Some of the handsome 17th century cottages which lined it still stand on the west side of Bath Street. The name probably derives from the native rock (Old English, rocc) with which it was paved.

Otherwise, the way lay through St. John's Churchyard, then containing houses and an inn, the Bell, and up Gentle Street. This was the former Hunger Lane, also known as Small Street. The first mention of Gentle Street is in 1698 but a Gentle family lived in the street (at no. 7) in the 16th century. It seems that many of these street names were used in speech long before they became accepted officially and so appeared in documents.

Joseph Clavey avoided all these steep streets by starting his 'flying waggon' in 1744 from Clavey's Barton which led into Behind Town (Christchurch Street East). This was later called Church Lane and when the lock-up was built in the corner of St. John's churchyard, as Blindhouse Lane, the lock-up being without a window. The name persisted.

Shortage of space prevents me dealing with Frome's many other old streets but a more comprehensive account will be found in the author's Frome Place-Names: Their Origin and Meaning, published by the Frome Society for Local Study.

CHAPTER 8

AN OUTSTANDING
EDUCATION

— Leslie White —

Frome and its surrounding district has always been in the vanguard of educational development. Enlightened landowners, business and especially church leaders established schools and educational foundations which are still reflected in the learning provision for people of all ages in the area today.

As we approach the beginning of the twenty-first century the town has an educational system organised and controlled by the members of the community which continues to develop and build on the solid foundations of the past and the best practice of the present.

The educational reforms introduced during the final years of the twentieth century have been very largely supported by the people of Frome and have given them the opportunity to create a system which is integrated and yet diverse, which is co-operative and yet competitive. At all stages from pre-school provision to age of thirteen there is a breadth of choice of learning opportunity available to parents and children which can be equalled in very few communities in the country.

While the school population is not large enough to sustain a choice of school after thirteen years of age, Frome Community College has been in the forefront of a movement in the local area to provide an integrated and co-operative way for all schools to deliver a unified approach to the National Curriculum for all the young people. This initiative of governors, teachers and headteachers to establish a federation of schools is unique to Frome and can only bring enormous benefits to the education of future generations.

There is a wide range of provisions for pre-school education in Frome with different organisations offering both full day and sessional day care for very young children. Two of the town's first schools have nursery units and there are eight other registered units giving full day care in the town, some catering for children with special needs. There are ten groups which offer sessional day care in the town and most of the villages provide some sessional day care. The opportunities for parental choice when children have to start their statutory education is equally wide and diverse.

There are small but well-resourced first schools in six villages; those at Beckington, Berkley and Mells are voluntary controlled Church of England Schools; Rode is a voluntary

Selwood school.

controlled Methodist School and those at Leigh-on-Mendip and Nunney are county schools.

The six schools in the town are larger and are also well-equipped: Christchurch and Trinity are both voluntary controlled Church of England schools; St John's is a voluntary aided Church of England school; Hayesdown and Vallis are county schools, while St Louis is a voluntary aided Roman Catholic school.

All these schools with their own individual foundations cater for pupils from the ages of four to nine years, except for St Louis, which provides for pupils from four to eleven when most children transfer to a Roman Catholic school in Trowbridge. At the age of nine all children have the choice of two large middle schools in Frome. Both these schools are amongst the largest in the whole country and this very fact ensures that the schools have specialist provision in teaching staff and in physical resources, giving Frome benefits of secondary schooling two years before the majority of pupils in England.

These two schools educate all the pupils in the area from the ages of nine to thirteen. Oakfield is a county school and Selwood a voluntary controlled school with a combined Church of England and Methodist foundation. At thirteen pupils transfer to Frome Community College, a thirteen to nineteen upper school which has additional provision on site for a wide variety of adult education.

Frome Community College has been a unique educational establishment since 1974 when it became a combined further education college and comprehensive school. It is now a designated Community College providing educational opportunities for all people in the area on one site at Bath Road. The first rate facilities, including the Merlin Theatre, a modern theatre seating 240, and the Frome Leisure Centre provide a campus which is designed to offer wide educational and recreational experiences to students of school age during the day and to students of all ages at other times. The commitment of Frome Community College to lifelong learning has created links with local groups, societies and sports clubs, placing it at a pivotal position in the creative life of Frome.

Critchill School is a special school which supports all the schools in the federation, as well as schools outside the Frome area. Critchill plays a vital role in the educational process, providing places for pupils with learning difficulties who are taught by specialists catering for specific individual needs in small classes. Pupils receive help as noted in their statements and are taught those parts of the National Curriculum relevant to their needs. In addition, Critchill is a Learning Support Centre providing books, equipment and materials for any concerned professional, and organising courses, particularly for teachers and classroom assistants.

All the schools in and around Frome have agreed to work together as the Frome Area Schools' Federation for the benefit of children in all three phases of education. There is a long tradition of collaboration between the schools, but in recent years the need for even closer co-operation was underlined by the introduction of the National Curriculum and the increased devolution of responsibilities to the local community. Liaison between governors and teachers is seen to be of the highest importance to ensure that the curriculum on offer to the pupils in the area affords each individual child the opportunity to achieve his or her potential in the National Curriculum, and to experience a wide and variable curriculum in which each stage builds on the achievements made at the previous schools.

The people of Frome and its surrounding district should be proud that so many members of the community are working together for the good of its young people. The continuing vision and remarkable co-operation of Frome's teachers in the last two decades have reaped the maximum benefit from our enlightened schools' founders. This is of tremendous benefit to our children, who have educational possibilities second to none.

CHAPTER 9

FROME CARNIVAL

— John Moxon —

In the third week of September, just after Frome Cheese Show, Frome has its great orgy, its Carnival. In the afternoon, children parade in the outfits their fond parents have so carefully prepared. Girls in pretty dresses and gowns, boys as Batman, Spiderman and many a skinny Superman are to be seen.

Wrapped up as Christmas parcels, pepper and salts; amazingly realistic Aladdins on their magic carpets, amuse us. Floats decorated by Sunday Schools, Youth Clubs, Mothers' Clubs, with the Junior and Senior Carnival Queens in the lead, the Children's Carnival procession winds between the crowds to the Park to be judged, and few go away without a prize.

Long before the evening procession is due to start, crowds begin to line the streets, and excited children persuade their parents to buy them brightly coloured balloons, luminous neck bands or toy trumpets, whose tinny sounds add to the expectant atmosphere.

Dead on time, (although the impatient crowds would never believe it!) the procession leaves its assembly point. Preceded by a loud speaker car entreating the crowds to give generously, the beautifully decorated floats of the Carnival Queens and their attendants are followed by a succession of floats which demonstrate the imagination of those that planned and constructed them, some, over many months.

Music plays loudly as each float passes, and nowadays they are all lit up, some by a magnificent array of light bulbs. There will be Chinese dragons, scenes from West End Plays, a float illustrating the Willow pattern, adults and/or children, beautifully costumed standing to attention for more than an hour, or performing a complicated dance routine.

Humour plays a large part in the Carnival, the several counter marching baton twirling troupes of prize-winning majorettes contrasted by some, surprisingly big-boned, whose hairy legs and over-blown busts betray their unlikely origins. The atmosphere is of great good nature and laughter abounds.

The collection is an important part of the Carnival, and organised efficiently by the Frome Rotary Club, with change-giving cars, collecting points, and it is helped by teams of collectors in every kind of garb; Scouts, Red Cross, youth clubs, and many individuals often in highly unlikely disguises, sell programmes and shake numbered collecting tins in front of the watching audience, bend down to patiently receive the coppers painstakingly put in the slots by tiny children, or carry buckets, ever heavier, full of collected coins.

Several collecting vehicles invite the public to throw their coins, bands play amongst the floats, expertly lead by Frome Town Band, and some counter-march in practised fashion. Ambulances, fire engines and trade vehicles swell the procession, which takes over an hour to pass. At the end, the collecting tins and buckets are gathered up and securely locked away for the night in a bank vault.

Next day, Sunday, at ten o'clock a band of Carnival Committee and their friends and children, and the Rotarians, gather at the Day Centre. For three hours, buckets of coins (wet if it has rained!) are emptied on tables and sorted into piles of pennies, twopennies, silver, bronze, pesetas, drachmas and a few notes. Eventually all is counted into bank envelopes and fill more than 30 blue bank bags. When complete a chain of collectors pass these very heavy bags to the waiting lorry; its springs sag noticeably. This moves on to the bank, where the chain of helpers pass the bags down into the bank's vaults.

Thomas the Tank Engine at the start of Children's procession.

With smiling faces, and mutual congratulations and thanks, the weary band make their way home to a late Sunday lunch, having learned by how much the total collection beat the previous year's. Some note wryly the irony of selling hundreds of packets of change to people who put it in collecting tins from which it is counted and returned to the banks. Carnival is over for the year, but the committee members will soon be attending their first meeting to organise the next year's event.

Mandarin theme on carnival float.

Of course, people take the Carnival for granted, giving scant thought to all the work put into it, or who does what. Even less have wondered how it all started, and I am indebted to Ken Miller for passing on to me facts he has gleaned of its early days.

Apparently, in the early hours of one morning in 1927, the night shift of a local factory were having a break and talking about their visit to Bristol's 'Rag Week'. Why not have one in Frome? A committee was set up and an event was held. The profit of £50 was divided between the Frome Victoria Hospital and the Queen's (District) Nurses.

In the next year, the 'Rag' was repeated, raising £60, divided in the same way. The following year it was decided to get the town more involved and to call it 'Carnival'. The first meeting was held at the Victoria Hospital, supported by representatives from the Rag Committee – Frome Rotary Club – Girl Guides – Friendly Society – Town Band and eventually these numbered over 40. The highlight was a raffle of a new Austin 7 car, value £140. The sum of £25 was donated by the Austin Motor Co, £15 from local subscribers, £75 from an anonymous donor, leaving £25 to be found by the committee.

They discussed such things as throwing a temporary wooden bridge over the river to improve access, vouchers (not money) as prizes, to be exchanged in local shops, a physical culture display, a ladies football match, baby show, Sunday concert, and Frome United Brewery providing a lorry to transport the Carnival King and Queen. Three months later the Carnival was held and produced a profit of £935 8s 11d, an astounding sum for those days, four and a half small cars would be worth nearly £30,000 at today's prices!

In 1932 the procession included an elephant loaned by Lord John Sanger's Circus, and in 1936 the Superintendent of Police raised no objections to collectors stopping cars on the outskirts of Frome for donations as long as they were not dressed in Highwaymen's or Robbers' costumes! Mr Johns offered to donate his week's holiday, collecting donations whilst touring Frome with his barrel organ. The Carnival continued annually until 1939, was discontinued during the war and started again in 1945. The Hospital and Nursing Association were still the main beneficiaries.

After the NHS was formed in 1947 it was decided to change the beneficiaries, and the Carnival Charities Trust was set up with five trustees, to disburse the income for charitable purposes in the area covered by the Frome Urban and District Councils. Arthur Cornish, who did so much for the Carnival for so many years was a great believer that those who spend other people's money should have sweated hard to collect it.

There have been many changes over the years, in 1952 British Rail put on a cheap day excursion to Frome and added a later train, and in the late sixties and early seventies a rag newspaper The Frome Rumour was a great success. In more recent years the Frome Rotary Club were asked to take over organising the collections as well as transporting the two Queens and attendants on their various commitments at events in the town.

Frome's popular Carnival will undoubtedly continue to entertain the crowds and provide funds to help local people in need. There will be changes, no doubt – one hopes for a return to the bigger local firms' sponsorship of large spectacularly decorated floats, and perhaps the public digging a bit deeper in their pockets for what is a very lavish bit of entertainment. Long may it flourish!

CHAPTER 10

COMMERCE TRANSFORMED

— Andrew Prince —

Commerce in Frome has over recent years undergone many changes and continues to do so quite dramatically in certain sectors. We have a greater than average number of people employed in manufacturing industry and, not surprisingly, a higher proportion than the national average of our workforce are involved in blue collar rather than white collar occupations.

It is clear from the recent recession that home grown industries have tended to survive much better and in some cases have grown in turnover and employment terms whereas subsidiaries of companies with head offices elsewhere have tended to be more prone to reduction of their workforce or even closure.

Because Frome is not situated close to the national motorway network and does not receive any regional grant aid it is difficult to attract new industry to the town. We have to rely on businesses established in the town developing and attracting satellite businesses who trade with them.

A perfect example is Mendip Foods which originally located its packaging section in Frome and then relocated their other departments from Wells and its head office from Bradford-on-Avon to North Hill House in Frome. In all they created over 250 jobs within our community.

J.R. Harding has worked with Mendip Foods and has grown with it, providing refrigerated transport and refrigerated storage facilities. It is now one of the country's leading specialist refrigerated food transporters and the red, blue and beige lorries can be seen all over the country advertising Frome to a wider audience.

Our District Council commissioned a survey of business and employment trends in Frome and as part of that asked businesses based in West Wiltshire what was their perception of Frome as a town and business centre.

One comment came through loud and clear and can best be summarised as Quality of Life. Frome is an unspoilt town. It is not covered by inner relief roads and largely retains its historic centre intact.

It is a pleasant place to live and work in. A contented workforce is pivotal to the success of business and something we should all remember when promoting our town.

Frome has four major sectors making up its business community and I make no apologies for starting with quarrying, which directly and indirectly represent one of our largest local employment groupings.

Quarrying and Mineral Extraction

Frome sits on the eastern end of the Mendip Hills and in an area bounded by Nunney, Whatley, Stoke St. Michael, and Doulting, limestone is quarried for use in the construction and road-making industries.

The major companies involved include ARC Southern, Foster Yeoman, Wimpey Hobbs and Cemas Aggregates.

The quarrying industry in the Mendips currently produces 13 million tonnes per year, of which over 7 million tonnes is delivered annually by rail.

More than 2,500 people are currently employed in quarrying and associated activities in the Mendips. There are many more jobs in support and service businesses, such as engineering, which are also dependent on the industry.

Total annual revenue of the Mendip quarries is around £150 million of which £40 million goes directly into the local economy through employee income and their expenditure with local suppliers.

Industry

Frome provides 25% of all jobs within the Mendip District Council area. Clearly our large employers play a very important part in the process both directly and indirectly through associated support services.

Frome currently has 11 businesses employing more that 100 people.

ARC Pipes, based at Mells, produces concrete pipes for the construction industry.

ARC Southern has its head office at Stoneleigh House, Frome, and local quarry at Whatley.

Bussmann Cooper UK is based at Garsdale, Frome, and specialises in the production of fuses and other small electrical components.

Butler & Tanner is Frome's largest employer with over 450 staff based at Caxton Road, and specialises in quality four colour printing and book binding, its quality productions are known throughout the world.

Cuprinol is based at Adderwell, Frome, and produces a wide range of wood preservatives.

Eden Vale, a subsidiary of Northern Foods, is based at Old Ford and from its modern plant produces processed milk products for the retail trade.

Foster Yeoman, with head office based at the recently restored Marston House, has its local quarry at Merehead, Downhead.

J.R. Harding group operates a specialist fleet of refrigerated delivery lorries. It also operates the Wessex Cold Store on the Marston trading estate.

J.R. Harding and Sons. Their modern factory at Wessex Fields.

Mendip Foods has its head office based at North Hill House, the former district council offices which were magnificently restored and reopened last year. They have a factory specialising in maturing and packing cheese for the food industry. Mendip Foods over the last three years has relocated a number of its satellite operations into Frome.

J.W. Singers currently operates on a site in the town centre although talks continue on relocation to a more suitable site. Singers specialises in bronze casting and foundry work.

Western Vinyls, a subsidiary of the EVC Group, is based in Vallis, Frome, and is a leading manufacturer of pvc sheeting.

Four of our largest industries employing in total over 1,000 people are locally owned and have group head offices based in Frome.

We must not forget the hundreds of smaller businesses in Frome providing an enormous range of goods and services. Over 12% of all people of working age in Frome are self-employed.

Service Industry

The term Service Industry covers businesses that provide a service but neither manufacture or resell a manufactured product.

Frome has an active service industry. In finance all four major banks have branches with resident managers. There are also five accountancy practices, seven estate agents, four insurance brokers, three architects and five solicitors within the town centre.

In tourism, Center Parcs, based at Longleat four miles from Frome, has created over 700 jobs, half of which have come from the Frome area.

In fact employment within the whole service sector grew by 32% in the period 1981 to 1991. All indications are that this sector will continue to provide more jobs within Frome.

Retailing

Frome along with many other market towns has seen substantial changes in retailing within the town centre.

Frome has a number of national multiples represented in the town centre, including Woolworths, Boots, Argos, and Martins. These are backed by a very good range of specialist local retailers.

Supermarkets are represented by Somerfield and Safeways in the town centre, both of which have recently undertaken expensive refits and a new 25,000 sq. ft. Sainsburys opened on an edge of town site at Wessex Fields in 1993. It was the opening of Sainsburys store that created the catalyst for change within the retail community.

The success of Sainsburys has lead to pressure on retailing within the town centre.

This has in turn led to a variety of changes and proposals to alter and vastly improve the services within our town centre. If only some of these come to fruition the retailing mix in Frome town centre will be greatly enhanced. These proposals and their impact are discussed at greater length in 'Frome, the Future'.

In conclusion commerce in Frome is alive and well. The unemployment rate has declined by 4% in the last three years. Manufacturing industry remains strong against the national trend, the service sector is growing rapidly and retailing, despite set-backs, is at the forefront of some exciting changes in our town centre.

CHAPTER 11

THE MEMORIAL THEATRE

— Derek Harman-Trick —

This is a success story that defies all logic. The Theatre was originally built in the 1920s, in the form of an 'active memorial' in memory of local citizens who died in the First World War. Unfortunately the funds ran out, and its uncompleted front was never finished, leaving its appearance less than satisfactory. With the changes in the entertainment industry the Theatre was leased as Frome's second cinema and ran successfully. However the cinema-going populace shrank away in Frome as everywhere else, with the coming of TV and the cinema closed. A period as a wrestling and bingo hall followed, then it fell into disuse.

Every year, however, it proved itself ideal for Frome's Amateur Operatic Society, whose shows were always a sell-out. Apart from this special use, the purpose-built 550 seat traditional theatre – complete with raked stage, flying curtains and orchestra pit, was getting little use. In the 1960s Frome Town Council invested the money it got from selling its Waterworks in building a modern 'hexagonal shaped' multi-purpose function room to the rear of the main building, but this did not succeed in rejuvenating the usage of the theatre, and it all deteriorated badly.

Little interest was shown by the public until the threat of demolition was raised. There was a lively public reaction, with pros and cons for the demolition. However the cons proved more vocal, and eventually an independent volunteer management team from the business community, was formed. They produced a ten-year business, fund-raising and restoration programme, against a lot of public disbelief. The town Trustees agreed and under the status of a charitable trading company, where all revenue is returned for the restoration campaign, the theatre opened for business to a huge emotional response from the public.

The facilities secured and all the plans introduced, they remain on schedule. Trading as The Memorial Theatre Complex, the company is a vibrant operation. It offers an all-the-year-round programme of 'variety' in the Theatre. Also, in the adjacent Assembly Rooms – with its superb professional catering team – up to 200 people can be accommodated for meetings, receptions, cabaret evenings and social functions. Two brilliant Glen Miller Orchestra evenings were long talked about and could have been booked twice over. It is already booked for next year.

Artistic impression of new frontage of Memorial Theatre and garden.

Already a number of organisations are using the facilities as 'home base', including the 'Operatic'. Regular blood donor sessions are booked and firms are starting to book the complex for staff training sessions. In the short time the complex has been opened, the bookings are coming in at an encouraging rate.

This success story against all odds is due to the vision and practical planning of the management team, the hard work of our many volunteers and the support of the public who are delighted 'their' theatre has been saved. The story ends satisfactorily with work starting on a memorial garden in front of the theatre and its appearance will be greatly enhanced by its splendid new frontage and enlarged foyer and bar.

CHAPTER 12

FARMING

— *Arthur Court* —

It was once said that 'Frome was the sort of town where one could buy a cloth cap'. This may be true, but the cloth used to make the cap was the key to the town's prosperity. Frome was a 'wool' town with two busy mills producing cloth as late as the 1930s.

The wool produced from flocks of sheep on the Wiltshire Downs and the Mendips was the raw material for the cloth. The River Frome provided the water for power, washing, and weaving the cloth.

While wool was an important part of local agriculture, milk production was the main source of income for the hundreds of family farms on the heavy clay lands in and around the town.

Until the advent of the Milk Marketing Board, in 1933, most of the milk produced was made into cheese on the farms, often by the farmer's wife. My own mother made cheese for most of her working life and, with some help in the house, reared five children. She also did a share of the hand milking. Frome became an important focus for cheese fairs, held at the Market Hall, which stands in the town centre, from which tons of cheese were sold to buyers from all over Britain.

While cheese fairs are a thing of the past, the Annual Cheese Show in September attracts an increasing number of cheeses, mostly made in factories. The real farmhouse-made cheese is almost a thing of the past. The organised marketing of milk made possible by the Milk Marketing Board in the 1930s put an end to farmhouse cheese production as it used to be.

Milk was collected from farms and directed to the most lucrative markets by the board. In the early days it was carried in churns each holding about 10 gallons. The churn has now been consigned to the museum to be replaced by refrigerated tankers holding several thousand gallons.

The agricultural industry has made remarkable progress in recent years by mechanisation and technological development. So much so that the land has yielded too much food. The problem in recent years has been how to reduce production. This has, to some extent, been brought about by our membership of Europe and the Common Agricultural Policy, which was designed to encourage food production.

In 1983 it was decided to introduce quotas for milk production. This has resulted in a

Champion of Frome Show.

market in quota sales and leasing at prices which make it almost impossible for newcomers to embark on milk production. The move towards lower output of food has been extended to cereal crops, and growers are paid to 'set aside' areas of land which must not be cropped. All farmers must now make returns to the Ministry of Agriculture on IACS forms if they wish to claim under the Arable Area Payments scheme. These returns have to include maps of each farm detailing crops or 'set aside' on every farm.

In exchange for this an extra payment is made on the reduced area under crops. In order to further reduce the output of food from our farms a new word has been coined, 'diversification' is the name of the game. Farmers are encouraged to introduce alternative uses such as golf courses, sporting and other activities to their land.

However, in spite of all this – or perhaps because of it, farming at present is in a fairly sound financial position. It is of concern that a large part of farming income is derived from subsidies and handouts which are in the control of Brussels and the Common Agricultural Policy.

Frome has always been a market town. The old livestock market in the centre of the town served well enough in the horse era, but as motor vehicles got bigger it became essential to move out of the town to a larger and more accessible site. This move has proved a great success and is described in detail elsewhere.

What of the future? So much now depends upon the policy for European agriculture. We can compete successfully, if we have a level playing field. The problem of animal welfare will not go away and the export of live animals is likely to remain a concern.

The growing cult of vegetarianism is likely to reduce the consumption of meat. We shall see a rise in demand for free range eggs and for meat reared and fed out of doors. British farmers have nothing to be ashamed of in their treatment of animals. The question is whether we can influence the rest of Europe to follow our lead.

One thing is certain, farmers must produce what the customer wants and customers are becoming ever more discerning.

CHAPTER 13

500 INTERESTING
BUILDINGS

— Michael McGarvie —

There are more than 500 buildings in Frome considered by the Government to be of 'Architectural or Historic Interest'. The 'interest' in some cases is marginal and other buildings have been included for their group value. Nevertheless, with such richesse we can deal only with a sample here. Because of the great rebuilding in the 17th and 18th centuries (not to mention Victorian refronting) mediaeval Frome has little to show for itself.

It is usually the churches which are ancient, but the 19th century restoration of St. John's was so thorough that little of mediaeval structure survives. Rightly, it is renowned not for its Saxon stones or Norman archways but as 'a perfect example of high Victorian architecture'.

A majestic interior is let down by an insipid west front and perhaps the most unusual feature is the Via Crucis, sculptured representations of the stations of the cross with Christ's crucifixion on the north porch, an astonishing object in an Anglican churchyard.

The Old Presbytery at the end of Cork Street, housed the first Roman Catholic church in 1850 and retains the vestiges of a mediaeval priest's house.

The most evocative relic of Frome in the Middle Ages, however, is the ruined bridge at Murtry with its fine chamfered arches and bold ribs gently decaying amid foliage and murmuring waters.

As one would expect, some of the most ancient and interesting houses in Frome are in Cheap Street. Once nicknamed 'The Pepper Pot' no. 13 (today A.T. May) with its high-pitched, stone-tiled roof, claimed to be the oldest house in the town, but this distinction belongs more properly to no. 11 (Amica) with its jetties, or overhanging storeys (the lower one filled in) and massive beams carved with Tudor rosettes. It and several of its neighbours go back to the 16th century as a stroll down Apple Alley to view their backsides – a true walk into the past – quickly confirms.

In Cork Street, Monmouth Chambers, recently well restored by Mrs. D. Brown, dates from close to 1600 and retains a handsome newel staircase and ornamental plasterwork in ceiling and frieze.

Coaches waiting at Frome's Brunel designed railway station in 1900. Bull's Hotel became the Post Office.

It was here that the Duke of Monmouth stayed in 1685 on his way to defeat at Sedgemoor and ultimate execution, one of Frome's few close links with national historical events.

Gentle Street is rich in 17th century houses whose gables – seven in all – are a hallmark of the town. The Hermitage and The Chantry were formerly one house with extensive gardens to fore and rear, so grand that it was wrongly said to be the Marquess of Bath's town house. The drawing room and master bedrooms, in The Hermitage are probably the most beautiful in Frome, while The Chantry has a notable dry larder of vaulted ashlar, often romantically referred to as a priest's hole.

There is also said to have been a priest's hole at no. 10 Gentle Street, owned by Lord Stourton in 1692 when Richard Tucker lived there. Tradition speaks of a secret panel and underground steps leading off towards St. John's. The Waggon and Horses was an inn from 1568 until 1960.

The wool trade in Frome was exceedingly prosperous around 1700 and several of the town's finest buildings are of this vintage. The most notable is Rook Lane Chapel, the work of a local builder, James Pope, and costing £300 in 1707. With its great pediment, two tiers of symmetrical windows and noble doorcase, it looks more like one of those

fashionable mansions which were going up at the time than a place of worship.

That the model was a heathen temple seems to have escaped the Congregationalists who commissioned the building. The chapel is imposing rather than beautiful and the same may be said of the interior with its mighty Doric columns and timbered dome.

Rook Lane is a Grade 1 building of national importance as is the Blue House, erected in the 1720s and at £1401 8s 9d rather more costly to build. It endears by reason of its 'disjointed' design with its excellent classical centre which housed the school combined with prosaic wings with old-fashioned mullioned windows and great chimney stacks rising up their facades. In these lived the almswomen and the paupers, each in their wing; between existed a social divide of unfathomable depth.

An attractive house of similar date is 13, Bridge Steet where the market bailiff lived. Its show front strives for classical sophistication but instead achieves an individuality and bucolic charm which make it an architectural delight.

Melrose Lodge in Whittox Lane is an altogether more serious example of Georgian symmetry. Its windows were originally transomed and mullioned, but later in the 18th century sashes were inserted in the front to be in the fashion. Inside is a good staircase and elegant panelled rooms, some painted with land – and seascapes.

The Keep in Castle Street is an example of a late 17th century house with a front added about 1750. It is unique of its date, being composed of small bricks laid in English Garden Bond, mellow and lovely. Brick was an unusual building material in Frome at that time.

North Hill House, nicely restored by Mendip Foods, was designed by William Jesser, an amateur architect, about 1760. Its original elegance has been rather spoilt by top-heavy Victorian additions.

Argyll House in Gentle Street, so-called after the duchess who lived there in 1855, is well-known for its splendid 'Chinese Chippendale' staircase. Mary Jesser commissioned it in 1766.

The mansion's pattern book array of Venetian windows complement those of West Lodge in Christchurch Street West which, far from being Lord Bath's hunting lodge, was the doctor's house in Frome for more than 200 years. It was erected in 1778. These houses of somewhat conventional Georgian design, were followed in the 1780s and 1790s by those in the Adam

Gentle Street, Frome. Showing late 17th century houses with Georgian sash windows and embellishments above a roadway paved with setts. From the left: The Chantry, The Hermitage, The Waggon and Horses. A railing in front of the Hermitage is mentioned in Court Rolls in 1698.

style with their delicacy of form and decoration represented in Frome by Fromefield and Mendip Houses (the latter in Welshmill Road) and by College Place in Wallbridge.

Adam's vogue was short lived; Frome discarded it and adopted the Gothic revival with some enthusiasm. Three charming examples of the Gothic cottage-orne' style survive in Garston Farm, Selwood Lodge and Innox Hill Cottage, all built about 1820.

A curious instance of spiky Gothic, an unscholarly but attractive Early English manifestation, is Holy Trinity Church, completed in 1838. It was designed by H.E. Goodridge, of Bath, who did not trouble to view the site. Nevertheless, his spirelets made a good show from Trinity Street.

Inside the church are Morris & Co. windows inspired by Burne-Jones. Later Gothic varies from the Old Police Station in Christchurch Street West (1856) whose architect was Major C. Davis, to the neighbouring Wesley Buildings (1863) by W.J. Willcox, a much more spirited design which must have been an eye-catcher from Bath Street before the trees grew up.

Via crucis, "an astonishing object in an Anglican churchyard".

In Portway is Joseph Chapman's fanciful Gothic cottage of 1867 with tracery, carvings and angle windows with colonettes. Chapman, an architect and builder, was also responsible for the Selwood Printing Works erected in the Byzantine style from 1876, and the Italian romanesque facade of Zion Chapel, Whittox Lane, in 1888.

These may be compared with the Literary and Scientific Institute in North Parade where in 1868 J. Hine adopted a round-windowed Venetian mode with prominent balconies, and the Masonic Hall opposite where local surveyor P. Edlinger chose a subdued neo-Egyptian style in 1891. Frome architects were nothing if not eclectic!

Relics of Frome's industrial past have not survived well, but much remains of Wallbridge Mill with its handsome brick dyehouse constructed by Alfred Tucker in 1887, now spoilt by modern cladding.

Eighteenth century drying 'stoves', stone towers used to dry dyed cloth, remain, one in Willow Vale and another in Justice Lane. The latter has been restored (architect David Short) as the tourist office.

Frome Railway Station is also notable having been built in 1850 and designed in the office of Brunel. It retains in use its overall roof, a rare feature. These are just a very few of Frome's many interesting buildings whose individual detailing and variety of style do so much to reward a browse round its ancient streets.

CHAPTER 14

WHAT DO FROME'S FUTURE POPULATION THINK?

— *Editor* —

It seemed sensible in a book concerned about the future of Frome, to find out what interested young people would like to see in the town most of them are going to live in. So we ran an essay competition for under nineteen and under thirteen year olds, entitled 'The Frome I would like to live in.' We had a marvellous response and I am grateful to the teachers who kindly set it up. You will have the pleasure of reading the winning entries in this book. Congratulations to the two winners, Chris Eales and Jessie Taylor, and the other prize winners! It was most interesting to read all the essays. I feel readers will like to know what suggestions recurred constantly, there must be a lesson for us amongst them.

Over and over again the writers complained that there appeared to be no communication of 'the Council's' deliberations. Sometimes it seemed to be the Town Council, and sometimes the District Council that was being attacked, and councillors were credited with very little sense! They were not believed to have considered the most obvious solutions. I am certain that both the children and the councillors would benefit from occasional but regular question and answer sessions at the schools, so that the very interested children are better informed. They might even correct the parents from whom I suspect they got some of their ideas! Four writers brought up the oft repeated local fiction that 'the council' turned down Marks & Spencer's at some time. I am assured that this is untrue and that if the population increased to 90,000, this excellent firm would be interested, and 'the council' would be delighted.

A further surprise for me was the most repeated complaint. It was about Frome's litter and generally dirty state. If children start to complain of the dirt they see around them, then it clearly needs attention! I suspect the impression of dirt comes from the dreadful state of the run-down Westway Precinct in recent years, with its generally drab and uncared for appearance, uneven paving stones, blocked drains and garish overdone posters in some of the shops. By the time this book is published, the Westway Precinct will look very different. The number of supermarket trolleys thrown into the river by the bored, the idle and the intellectually unchallenged, has reduced since at long last they have been chained up and

Frome's champion Town Crier, Steve Haberfield.

charged for. The cleaning up of the town, is probably the cheapest of the suggestions received, the Town Council is already paying for extra help, and may be more is needed.

The next most popular suggestion was for a music shop, HMV being mentioned by four optimists. The empty shops were noted, and the lack of clothes shops and chain stores in a traffic-free centre complained about. Places to meet and chat for young teenagers – those below the age of going to pubs – was a frequent suggestion, coffee bars and other meeting places with an adult presence to prevent bullying being suggested. The young people were concerned at the police station being frequently closed and felt that more police to be seen on the streets would improve their town. The latter comment, made by adults, is frequently heard up and down the country, but if you read Inspector Gazzard's article, you may feel some reassurance about the local situation.

Several asked for improved sports facilities, especially at Victoria Park, where the disappearance of the goal posts was complained about. Unemployment and the environment were, of course, of great concern; many thought the town divided in two by the lack of a common 'meeting place' in the centre, and what surprised me more than anything, being used to being told by experts what young people think, was their frequently expressed appreciated of Frome's old buildings and streets.

Any town inviting its opinionated youth to write about improvements they would like to see will get a lot of criticisms. I am encouraged by the comparatively small number of such complaints about Frome, the fact that several of the improvements suggested are already well in hand, and that most of the others are manageable from a small budget. I strongly believe that a determined effort must be made to continue cleaning up the town, that several coffee bar type places should be opened, possibly subsidised to begin with, and sports facilities at Victoria Park be improved. We surely owe this to our young people, for whom we are unable to provide the degree of employment they are entitled to expect. I cannot believe that the presence of and cost of dealing with vandalism and crime is a better alternative.

It was a real pleasure to find that most of the young people said how much they liked living in Frome, and thought that their improvements, if carried out, would make Frome the best possible place to live in .

FROME, THE TOWN I WOULD LIKE TO LIVE IN

Winner, under 13 Essay Competition

— Jessie Taylor —

I think family facilities are one of the main things potential buyers look for when choosing a house. Therefore I feel the following improvements should be made in Frome: firstly, it would be a lot easier for parents to shop without their children. It would not cost a lot to set up a creche in the centre of town. It would be well used and could be run by volunteers who were interested in child care.

Secondly, in most places it is very hard to find baby changing facilities. There are several cafes and shops which have space, but just need that extra bit of money to convert it into baby/disabled facilities.

Thirdly, we need an extension built on to the swimming pool including water chutes which would attract families from far away. This is good for people with children because it would be something for them to do at the weekend.

Fourthly, a young persons' cafe open in the evenings where teenagers could meet and buy snacks would attract people with older children along with a non-alcoholic bar for all ages. This would be very appropriate for persons under 16 and adults that would prefer to drink in a non boozy, pleasant atmosphere.

Fifthly there are lots of places in town that could be renovated into workshop spaces for young people to set up businesses and to practice music etc. They could be hired out or rented. This would help people to keep themselves off the street.

In the evenings Frome is deserted. If the river and bank were cleaned up people could set up boating businesses, boat cafes and riverside cafes. In the summer there would be lots of opportunities ranging from outdoor music to an open-air craft market. The stalls in the market could be made up of people who run the local bric-a-brac shops and any people from the market e.g. jewellery stalls.

At the moment Victoria Park has quite an aggressive atmosphere. Because of all the children that hang around the skateboard ramps, people do not feel that it is safe to leave their younger children there. There is also nowhere where you can get a drink. People have to bring cans when they come, adding to the litter around. If there was a cafe and a warden it would give the park a much more relaxed, safe feeling.

FROME, THE TOWN I WOULD LIKE TO LIVE IN

Runner up, under 13 Essay Competition

— *Anna Simms* —

I have lived in Frome all my life, and there are lots of changes I would like to see. The first thing that I feel needs to be changed, is to make it cleaner; make it a litter free zone, with litter bins on every street, to cut down high pollution rates. Apart from the litter, dog waste on pavements and on Frome's streets needs to be sorted out. I think that 'Doggie' waste bins on every street could cut down dirty, messy, town streets. If penalty notices were up, then this would encourage dog owners to use the bins. Other ways of making Frome clean, are to have more council maintenance — things such as sweeping the streets regularly, and weeding along gutters and pavements.

Throughout Frome, I feel there are too many antique shops and charity shops. I like to see charity shops, but I do think Frome has too many, and I would like to replace charity/antique shops which don't gain enough trade. I think Frome would benefit from decent clothing shops for all ages, not too many, because this is expensive, but it would bring a lot of trade to Frome. The boarded up shops up Catherine Hill need to be restored to accommodate these businesses.

When I have free-time, I feel there isn't a lot to do in Frome, and other youngsters feel the same. I think that there should be a young person's cafe or meeting place, with reasonable prices, and promoting a healthy life style, especially for youngsters in the ages between 10-15.

To try to cut down the crime rates, I feel that more policemen need to be on patrol around the town.

Finally, to encourage all ages to be sporty, and to keep youths off the streets, better sports facilities should be provided in Frome with an adventure swimming pool to attract youngsters, to make Frome an enjoyable town for everyone.

FROME, THE TOWN I WOULD LIKE TO LIVE IN

Third, under 13 Essay Competition

— Andrew Pattison —

By the year 2000 I would not like to see Frome as it is now. For a start Catherine Hill, which used to be the centre of Frome's business life has now deteriorated to a deserted street with just a few hardy shops and businesses remaining. The desolated street with shop windows boarded up and the empty remains remind me of a dream, or nightmare even.

So in the year of the new millennium I would like to see a new side of Catherine Hill. A street full of people bustling to get in shops which are full of cheap high quality products that sell very well, leaving the shops with enough money to expand and grow all over the country.

Secondly, I think that Frome needs something different from just another town in the country. Perhaps something historically important, or perhaps we just need something to happen here, good or bad, so as to have the name of Frome in the back of everybody's mind. Given the chance to live in Frome, many would jump at it rather than going to live into another town or in the local cities such as Bath or Bristol where most of the work is.

After the move of hundreds of M.O.D. jobs to Bristol many who live in Frome who already had a long trip to Bath every day will probably not want to drive any further north in to North Bristol. So, many of them will move into Bristol and take even more business away from Frome, which is definitely not what it wants at the moment.

Frome really needs to deal with its crime problem. Too much vandalism and car crimes occur in Frome and by the year 2000 I hope that Frome's problems will have nearly deceased from normal life in and around Frome. To tackle this problem, I think two things need to be done.

1. I think that if the adults, police and maybe children themselves educate other children from a young age about crime, crime would go down dramatically.

2. I know, from what people at the same age as me have said, that if there was more in Frome for young people to do then crime also would reduce.

Personally, I think that coming from a small village, young people have a great deal to do, such as all the sports and clubs at the Sports Centre, the many youth clubs, even after school clubs can occupy young children's and teenagers' time. But that's where the problems come. I don't think that there are enough activities for older teenagers so they don't spend their time, wasting others'.

I also think that some of the parks in Frome such as Victoria Park and the Welshmill playground need a face lift, with new equipment such as a few new swings and such like. Overall, I think Frome needs more businesses so as to increase its sphere of influence over the country and be known up and down the country.

FROME, THE TOWN I WOULD LIKE TO LIVE IN

Winner, under 19 Essay Competition

― *Chris Eales* ―

There are many good points which need to be said about Frome. These include the tourist information centre, which shows visitors to Frome just what Frome is about. The new car park by the library brightens the centre of Frome and is a good place for tourists and visitors to park.

A good idea for Frome would be to replace the redgras pitch at the Sports Centre by an astroturf one. It would be better for the college and the community; it would allow many more sports to be played in that area of Frome, for example tennis courts, basketball courts and a proper running track and athletics. It would be much more used.

The monuments/historic buildings in and around Frome that have been cleaned, look good, for example Rook Lane Chapel could and probably will be a major tourist attraction to Frome after the cleaning that has been undertaken.

Generally, the Town Council has been doing a good job, keeping Frome up to national standards. But, as always, things could be improved; many ideas are outlined below:

Many lovely buildings are in and around Frome town centre, many of which could be cleaned and made even more marvellous. Which, hopefully, could attract more business to this area.

Another idea could be a careers centre combined into the tourist information centre. Maybe another good idea would be cycle paths around the Frome countryside to help the Frome public keep more healthy and also be an environmental bonus in travelling by bike to places. To attract more tourists/visitors to Frome maybe some picnic sites dotted around Frome and signposts showing places for tourists to stay at whilst visiting the Frome area and bringing money.

For Frome's public, maybe an upgrade of the redundant buildings at the side of the new carpark into a mini-shopping precinct for more business to come to Frome. In this mini-shopping precinct could be a council-owned shop where the public could sell home made local produce.

Then, to upgrade Frome's image as a caring town, the council could put up flagpoles along the bridge by the Blue House in the centre of town. On these flagpoles a flag showing Frome's shield to promote Frome and to welcome visiting tourists. Maybe a few more trees and flowers around Frome to make Frome a nicer and more pleasant place to stay.

FROME, THE TOWN I WOULD LIKE TO LIVE IN

Runner up, under 19 Essay Competition

— *Leeandra Curtain-Marten* —

In Frome I think we should have more variety, for young children in Frome, because if we did it would attract other people from villages to come to Frome. We could put some activities where there are some spare shops which aren't being used. Maybe a young people centre where people could socialise there and have lots of discos and clubs. For young people in Frome there is nothing much to do, so people go around vandalising and causing grief. And for the older people maybe a bingo and or coffee bar where they could go to socialise.

In Frome we could do with a clothes shop; we have got one but some old people and middle-aged people won't use it, because it's for young people. In Frome, in Catherine Hill, there are lots of old shops which are just empty and Frome are building new shops instead of using the old ones. In Frome I think they should improve Victoria Park; lots of different age people enjoy Victoria Park, maybe more activities on the grass, and more entertainment. I think also the sports centre could be expanded by different activities, more activities in the day, and the evening.

I think Frome is a very nice town, and also well organised but if we advertised Frome for its good points, more people would visit Frome. If Frome had some more flowers and other things added to the town it would brighten up Frome to show what a nice clean town it really is.

FROME, THE TOWN I WOULD LIKE TO LIVE IN

Runner up, under 19 Essay Competition

— Ken Vernon —

The Frome I would like to live in, has a sense of community, with lots of whole community projects, linking the two halves of our town.

Also, the town would be prosperous, and industry would be thriving, with large name chain stores, mingling with the smaller, family/local businesses. Also there would be more things to occupy our time with, for all age ranges, from sports facilities, to night clubs, to more family orientated things, such as cinemas or theatres.

All of these shops and entertainment facilities would be spread throughout the town, not just centred in the town's centre or in one area. This would give the entire community benefit from any improvements, and force people from different parts of the town, to mingle with each other.

There are many places in Frome, where such projects could take place. One of which is the old Colorol building near Wallbridge, which has been empty for many years now. Or even the old ARC depot. Both of which could house a large department store, or as has been previously proved, a factory.

Both of which would fit into Frome very comfortably, as with our fairly large population, we could sustain a large store, with relative ease, and we have quite a large section of unemployed people, so a large factory would do no end of good, to the economic situation of many people in the area, and indeed the town as a whole.

The other main change in my Frome, would be a general clean-up of the town centre. This would encourage people to come into Frome, from outside the area, instead of them going to other towns and cities, like Trowbridge, Bath or Bristol.

This could be achieved by creating a new shopping area in the town, which would be pleasant to walk around, so would be respected by those who used it. This has been proven by the enclosed shopping centre in Trowbridge, the 'Shires', which manages to stay clean and tidy, due to the respect it gets because of its cheerful atmosphere.

And that concludes the changes I would make to Frome, if I had the chance.

CHAPTER 16

FROME'S SURROUNDING VILLAGES

— *John Moxon* —

Frome, being a market town, has always been closely involved with its surrounding villages, providing shopping, employment, schools or communications for those who lived nearby.

Inevitably, with the continued marked decrease in employment on farms due to mechanisation, and the decline of the woollen trade, much of its work having been done in village mills and cottages, there has been a steady migration of people, especially the young, from the villages to the town. The reduced child population caused the gradual closure of village schools, which always seemed to leave the villages in a state of shock, temporarily, taking the heart out of them.

Inward migration of people from 'foreign parts', or, at least, from other counties, was at first bitterly resented; but in most villages, as the years have passed, the newcomers have joined with the 'locals' in helping the villages survive. They are on village hall committees, and help run the village fetes. Although, regretfully, the 'newcomers' have not created much local employment, and have caused the price of houses to rise above the pockets of the young workers of the village, as the latter have moved to the town, anyway, perhaps the villages have made a net gain.

Frome Selwood may have dropped the 'Selwood' from its name many years ago, but the old name is still carried on by the local parish which surrounds the town. Dennis Pattinson reminds me that the former outlaw territory of East and West Woodlands are still in Selwood, as are Tytherington, Egford, Vallis, Spring Gardens, Old Ford and Rodden. All attractive in their diverse ways, they make up, with adjoining Berkley, patterned corridors into Frome.

Fred Chant, who writes so entertainingly about village life, has told me about the close-knit village life of the Buckland Dinham of his youth, attending the local school till eleven and then moving on to Wesley School in Frome. His father had been a miner at the Radstock pit, and doing a host of other skilled jobs, including thatching, on top of a full day of the mining that was to kill him. The cheeses made in the village were well known till the practice stopped with the growth of the St Ivel Dairies at Old Ford. The closure of the

village school, he says, affected the village badly, the village lost its petrol pumps, shops and post office, but has always strongly supported its village hall, and Christmas pantomime. Charlie Downton's Fountain Inn was a cider house, once a centre of many people's lives in the village. It survived as a bit of an anachronism till recent times, and its demise left the pretty Bell Inn as the only pub.

A mile or so out of the village lies Ammerdown Park, the seat of Lord Hylton, with its beautifully restored garden. It houses a Catholic Retreat and Study Centre which is very active. Appearing through the trees is a 150 ft elegant pillar, a memorial to Thomas Jolliffe, MP.

Mells, three miles from Frome, is a particularly pretty village. Its interesting houses are scattered along a surprisingly large number of narrow lanes, well-worth exploring. The beautiful New Street was new in 1470 when built by Abbot Selwood, and leads to a lovely 16th century church, which includes memorials to Edward and Mark Horner, killed in World War I. They were the last of a well-known line, and featured in the children's rhyme: 'Little Jack Horner'. Lord Oxford and Asquith, a nephew, now lives in the Elizabethan Manor House. The simple but moving village war memorial is by Sir Edwin Lutyens, designer of the Cenotaph, in London's Whitehall. With an enterprising pub, post office, school and active village hall, the village is quite self-contained. It celebrates Spring with an Easter Daffodil Fair. Hundreds of thousands of daffodils delight the eye.

Nearby Great Elm is a small village which overflows down a very steep hill into a beautiful valley. A little stream borders the home of Maureen Lehane, the inspiration behind the increasingly popular Great Elm Music Festival, founded in memory of her husband the composer Peter Wishart. Other arts, including painting and pottery, as well as music, are championed at Jackdaws, a house at the end of her drive, converted into an art gallery by the late Mrs Rose Bugden.

The hamlet of Whatley is dominated by its church, unusual locally, for having a steeple, in it is the 14th century effigy of Sir Oliver de Cervington. Whatley also has a vineyard. A couple of miles further on lies Chantry whose houses are a mixture of old and new. Its church was an early design of Sir George Gilbert Scott for the Fussell family, famous manufacturers of edged tools, still to be found in the area. A bit further on, Leigh-on-Mendip is always mispronounced by visitors as 'Lee', but locally is joined up as 'Lion'. It has a church with a tall perpendicular tower, seeming almost disproportionate in such a small church. It is beautifully kept, with its many carved oaked pews and Norman font. The village looks as if it has remained peaceful since its last skirmish in the Civil War. It has a surprisingly ambitious pub, with skittle alley, a store, post office and school.

The ancient village of Nunney is the largest in the area. Its splendid moated castle, built in 1373 by Sir John de la Mere survived without being breached till the Civil War, when it survived the siege, by the deceit that it had a plentiful supply of fresh pork by the ruse

Left: A host of them at the Mells Daffodil Festival.

of pulling a young pig's ears and tail daily causing much squealing, until betrayed by a deserter. Parliament ordered the castle 'slighted' and so it remains to this day. Sir John's tomb survives in the interesting church nearby. A river flows prominently through the village, which has not only an ambitious flower show, but an excellent Nunney Fayre, necessitating closing the street all day. It has always had a flourishing school, and has a shop, post office, hairdresser and a residential home.

Travelling south through the small village of Trudoxhill, which has a large dining hall for hire and where the excellent pub brews its own ale and supplies several other pubs as well, we come to Witham Friary. An attractive collection of houses and farms are clustered around a series of bends on the way in and out of the village. It lost its school many years ago, but then had an influx of new people when three of its farms were sold, and came back to life again. Then it lost its shop and post office, but still manages a splendid annual fete in its central children's playing field. The old Carthusian Priory's remains are limited to the dovecote, now the parish room, and the church's unusual bell tower, recently restored, shows its three bells hanging in silhouette.

Turning right for a mile or so, one comes to the attractive village of Upton Noble, which is usually left out of the guide books, for some reason. Its once popular pub regretfully has closed, though there are still attempts to remedy this. It changed hands regularly, in the past four decades, and alternated between providing excellent food and atmosphere, and the reverse, till non locals gave it up, in confusion. A manor house is clearly visible from the attractive countryside around, and unlike most other villages, its school thrives, taking its pupils from many surrounding villages. It also has a garage.

Crossing the Bruton road, we come to the large village of Batcombe, in a valley below the rising Mendip Hills. It is remarkable for its many fine houses and gardens, and attracts people in retirement. It has a good pub, and a post office tucked away at one end of the very long village, which is dominated by its fine church, with a splendid tower built in 1543, it is one of the best amongst Somerset's renowned perpendicular towered churches.

Heading back towards Frome on the Bruton road, we pass through the small village of Wanstrow which is developed equally on either side of the road. As well as a good village hall, it boasts a pub, a garage and a large caravan centre. Nearer Frome the hamlet of Marston Bigot is all that remains of the former village, seat of the Bygot family in the 13th century, whose manor is only marked by the still visible moat in a field.

Taking the back road through Tytherington with its popular Fox & Hounds pub, travellers come to West Woodlands which is but a few houses on the main road. However, its twin East Woodlands is off the main road on the way to Longleat, and has a thriving church, (sharing the vicar of St John's Frome), and a refurbished village hall which is home to the 'Woodlanders' Music Hall which runs for 13 nights and is always a sell out for people from near and far.

Right: Nunney Castle.

— 66 —

Four miles down the road lies Maiden Bradley, just over the Wiltshire border, seat of the Duke of Somerset at Bradley House, and having a shop, post office, pub, and beautiful church, heralded by an avenue of pollarded trees and clipped yews. As well as beautiful Bradley House, there are several other fine houses in the village.

On to Horningsham, a lovely village; the houses are well spaced out over a considerable area. It has a school, post office, stores and a beautiful church. It also has a remarkable non-conformist chapel, the oldest in the country. The excellent Bath Arms is at the gates to Longleat Park.

Still in Wiltshire, on the other side of Longleat, and reached by passing the lovely and popular beauty spot of Heaven's Gate, reached down an avenue of rhododendrons, lies Corsley, which is a collection of hamlets: Lye's Green, Dertford (sic), Lane End, Temple, Corsley Heath, Sturford, Whitbourne Moor and Whitbourne Springs, Longhedge, Ringbourne, Gey's Hill, and Stalls. It is a large village of great variety. Narrow lanes with high walls lead into lanes with low hedges and lovely views. It has three churches and a manor house. Three pubs, a post office and a garage and shop, are found in this village divided by a busy main road, dominated in Summer by Longleat bound traffic, and once a year by the splendid Corsley Show.

Taking the back road from Corsley through a valley one climbs up to Chapmanslade which straddles the length of a hill and spills over the edges. A shop and post office has closed, but there are attempts being made to produce perhaps a part-time service. A popular pub and two nurseries bring life to this village with its busy community hall. Moving down the hill towards Frome and turning right we come to the tiny village of Berkley with its 'Wren' type church of 1751 against the manor house. The church has a decorated octagonal dome surmounted by a lantern. Its school's reputation draws pupils from well outside the village.

Passing the new Frome Market and on to Rode where the church tower stands out in the surrounding countryside. Its attractive lych gate had to go in the interests of safety as the busy Trowbridge road passes close by. Almost all the rest of the village is on the other side of the road; there is another distinctive church, alas recently closed because of the danger of collapse and there is a popular steakhouse restaurant. Its former manor house has the largest collection of exotic birds in the country, and is a popular place to visit and revisit, for children and adults.

On to Beckington, which is a big village with some fine seventeenth century (and perhaps earlier) houses. The handsome church has a Norman tower and the abbey has a superb plaster barrel-vaulted ceiling. Bishop Beckington of Wells was born in the village, which has returned to its earlier peaceful ways since the bypass took away almost all the traffic that charged through its centre. With two excellent pubs, one particularly renowned for its good food, a school, garage, craft shop, post office and grocers shop, it is well set up.

Left: St Giles Church, Leigh-on-Mendip.

Returning on the Frome road and turning right at Old Ford before its popular roadhouse, past the Staplemead Dairy, one comes to the delightful village of Lullington with a green surrounded by thatched cottages. Its early Norman church has an exceptionally fine north doorway and the most highly decorated Norman font in the county. One of the entrances to Orchardleigh park is outside the village. The mansion was built in the 19th century to replace the old manor house, but the gem is the 13th century church on an island on the lake, where Sir Henry Newbolt (and his dog!) is buried.

A drive through all these villages surrounding Frome is a delight, and takes about three and a half hours, allowing a visit to one or two of the churches. Far better to visit a few villages at a time and have time to enjoy them; they deserve it.

CHAPTER 17

EMPLOYMENT PROSPECTS

— Malcolm Williams —

As we edge towards the 21st century with what sort of shape will the town face the new millennium? If the last 50 years are anything to go by, a capability for change will need to be one of its assets. The 1980s saw a move from stagnation into boom, equally followed by one of the deepest recessions on record. Now, in 1995, the town is dusting itself down again and is getting back on track for steady recovery,

Still essentially a manufacturing centre, but what of the future for Frome? Will it cast off its artisan roots and traditional skills and enter a brave new world driven by information technology, or will its staple industries remain the keystones of the local economy? Neighbours, like Swindon, have waved goodbye to their railway heritage and new industries and commerce have flourished. Whatever the future of Frome, the capacity and ability to adapt must be one of the mechanisms.

Previous chapters pay homage to a town that can respond to change. My contribution looks at key areas like sectoral employment change, commuting patterns, trends in unemployment, training and enterprise advice, and what prospects there are for new inwards investment.

One of the quoted changes in the national economy was the relentless fall of manufacturing employment, and the progressive growth of service industry. At the time of the last census in 1991, just 21% of all those in employment worked in manufacturing.

In contrast in Somerset, manufacturing has retained its presence with over 26% of its workforce in the sector, while even more remarkably in Frome the figure is nearer 30%. However, the trend suggests that its importance is diminishing with a fall of 10% over the decade. In contrast service sector employment has grown by 32% in the district, and in Frome currently stands at about 60% of the total workforce.

What does this mean for Frome? It continues to have a disproportionately large manufacturing sector and is probably under represented in its white collar type opportunities.

What is the evidence? Undoubtedly, the town continues to be well represented by its major manufacturing employers, as Andrew Prince of the Chamber of Commerce has pointed out. A host of household names, 11 of which employ over 100 people, and the largest, Butler & Tanner, over 400. That these companies have sustained themselves during a tough recession is a testimony to their resolve and their forward thinking.

Part of the answer to Frome's maintenance of its industrial base has been a willingness to innovate and invest. Cuprinol, for example, has retained its market edge and developed an impressive export record by development of its product range. Much of it is now water based, and its range of wood preservatives are very much in tune with the environmentally conscious 1990s.

Its neighbour, Butler & Tanner has an impressive investment record. Engaging state of the art colour printing technology, and by an astute series of acquisitions, it has become one of the country's leading printers of hard backed books.

Mediaeval Wallbridge with, in the background, its riverside wool and carpet mill now a series of small business units.

In the face of such success, it is surprising that Frome is so self-effacing about its flagship employers. Perhaps it is because many of them are tucked away unobtrusively down quiet streets, and are simply happy to get on with their business. We should learn from our European neighbours in this respect and shout a bit louder about our industrial heritage. There is nothing inherently wrong in a civic pride that says 'Frome – home to the United Kingdom's largest printer of colour books'!

What of the future of Frome's manufacturing? Trends cannot be ignored, and my feeling is that actual numbers of jobs in the sector will continue to fall in the face of increased investment and productivity advances. This is not to say that in terms of GDP the sector will not continue to be important, and its staple industries be the bedrock of the local economy.

Turning to service industry, although under represented in the town, there is every sign that much of the future employment will be in this area. At present, Frome is not a major administrative centre like its near neighbour and Wiltshire's county town, Trowbridge. Its geographical location on the eastern boundaries of Somerset suggest that in terms of public administration, it will retain its status for area offices but not for major administrative functions.

So, if there is to be growth in the service sector where will it come from? I see two major areas. Firstly, retailing. After a tough five years in which this sector has been badly shaken locally, there are many signs that the corner has been turned. Initiatives for the town centre are starting to bear fruit, and the Government has at last acknowledged in its change of policy that out-of-town shopping has been unhelpful to town centre vitality. Frome has many of the attributes to build back its shopping capacity as it moves towards the millennium.

The great, unexploited industry locally is that of tourism. Frome, with its great heritage of fine buildings has been rightly identified by the Civic Trust as one of the most important undiscovered jewels of Georgian Architecture in the South West. Predictably, with a unique capacity for understatement, local people just take this for granted.

Tourism, like an industry, needs developing and managing. As the town centre regeneration gathers pace, tourism potential will need to be nurtured, and each small component of interest to the visitor, be it an individual building, or places to eat, must be presented in terms of quality of experience.

There is no better symbol of tourism than the establishment of the new Tourist Information Centre in the Round Tower. Apart from bringing back into use a derelict building, its success has confounded all the sceptics and has created a cluster of visitor activity around the Black Swan arts and craft centre adjacent to the market place.

Frome can, and has exploited the success of others. Foremost example is the futuristic and environmentally sensitive Center Parcs holiday village in nearby Longleat. The town's residents have greatly benefited already from many of the 700 plus jobs created there and it is well placed to capture the interest of visitors from Center Parcs looking to do something outside the village. Contrary to popular opinion, its patrons do venture outside its perimeter fences!

The reducing number out of work is a reliable measure of the buoyant state of the local economy. For too long in the 1990s, Frome sat on top of the unemployment statistics and not infrequently the town had the unwelcome attention of the national media in its doom and gloom coverage.

The picture has changed dramatically for the better. The most recent statistics show that unemployment has dropped down from high double figures to 8.1% (May 1995) and is now way down the league tables. Nonetheless, it is still too high, and the challenge is to find new sources of work for the 600 people still out of work.

What has led to the employment recovery? Clearly, the manufacturing industry has slowly started to recruit again, and small business activity is once again becoming more prevalent. Service sector growth, and major contributions from employers like Center Parcs have also played their part.

The 1980s saw a massive housing expansion and a commensurate growth of the local population. Many have claimed that Frome was becoming a dormitory town. What is the evidence?

Again, turning to that most reliable of sources, the Census, you must acknowledge that commuting is on the increase. In Mendip in general, commuting to employment sources outside the district increased by 48% over the last decade with an average of 23% of the workforce finding employment beyond its boundaries.

In Frome, the picture is mixed. On the northern side of the town in Welshmill and Fromefield, for example, between 25%–41% of residents work outside whereas in Badcox the average was nearer 20%.

It is not unhealthy that people look expansively for their work. No town can be self sufficient in employment. What is encouraging is that so many people moved to Frome in the 1980s because of what it has to offer. The challenge is to ensure that they use its amenities, and most importantly shop locally. Hence the improvements to the town centre.

Frome is well placed and accessible to several higher education establishments in Bristol and Bath and has a number of further education colleges only a short distance away. All are available for training and business advice.

There is no substitution, however, for town-based facilities, and the closure of the further education block at Frome College was a profound shock at the time. The need to better the training facilities in the town has also been identified since in the locally sponsored study on Frome's economy by internationally recognised consultants PA.

How can Frome respond? There is every sign that Frome College is looking to build back some of the lost ground, and is developing strong links with Strode College in Street. The college, far from expecting students, be they adults or teenagers, to travel to Street is developing ways of delivering training on site in Frome. Some of the first initiatives have been to help 'adult returners', particularly women, and courses have been oversubscribed.

Increasingly, in higher education the trend is towards 'distance learning'. With the greater use of networked computers and 'teleworking' local people will be able to study locally, yet link into first class establishments someway beyond the town.

On the business advisory side, Frome has had the benefit of its own local Enterprise Agency for the last 14 years. The Frome and Mendip Enterprise Agency (FAME) has provided a comprehensive range of services to small businesses, and has run a very successful Youth Training Scheme from which many local employers and youngsters have benefited.

FAME, too, is now poised to go into a new era. Nationally, the Government has pressed for single, comprehensive delivery points of advice for small businesses which were originally called 'One Stop Shops' now recast as Business Links Centres. FAME is poised

The press hall at Butler & Tanner, Frome's largest employer.

to reopen not only as Frome's Business Links office but will be the area office serving the whole of the Mendip area from its prestigious Vallis House premises.

Inward investment: however successful local business might or otherwise be, no location can afford to turn its back on opportunities from employers moving in from outside. To be successful, a town must in itself be attractive, have a well trained and motivated workforce, be accessible, and have a good supply of business land.

In the 1980s, the lack of new business sites in Frome had been the Achilles heel preventing any serious promotion of the town for business. It also inhibited the expansion of local enterprise. To combat this, the planners identified expansion land to the south west of the Marston Trading Estate covering some 20 acres. A further 10 acres was also identified between the old and new estates.

After much feverish activity, a new site – Wessex Fields – came on stream in 1989. It has attracted offices and a prestigious conference centre developed by IBS Limited, and eight acres has been taken by a new Sainsbury food store. Approximately eight acres remain.

More recently, a new link road joining Wessex Fields with the Marston Trading Estate has been opened which has facilitated the expansion of the local cold storage and haulage experts, J.R. Harding and Sons. The link road itself not only provides a higher quality access to the existing estate, but also opens up a further five acres of land.

There is little further scope for expanding the Wessex Fields area, and in readiness for the next phase of growth a further 40 acres has been identified off the Frome bypass at Coalway Lane. This high quality location has much to commend it as the next generation of business site for Frome.

Providing business land however, is only one side of the equation, there must also be good mechanisms for promoting an area. The West of England has until recently been severely disadvantaged because it could not compete on a level playing field with other parts of the United Kingdom for international inward investment.

As from September 1995, a new agency will be operational covering the counties of Somerset, Wiltshire, Dorset, Gloucestershire and Avon, funded locally and backed by the Government. It will have the same access to business inquiries as our arch-rivals South Wales and other regions of the United Kingdom. The West of England Development Agency (WEDA) is to adopt a proactive strategy for promoting the regions assets.

Will this benefit Frome? The best prospects for attracting new industry is to concentrate on our existing strengths on an original basis, and from this we must look to our sectorial advantages.

In Frome, we have two such assets. Firstly, the town's association with printing and allied trades is part of a wider cluster of like industries in Bristol and South Avon. Secondly, the food processing sector is well represented by the recent expansion of Mendip Foods and its associated cold storage and haulage capacity provided by Hardings. Eden Vale also retain massive milk processing capacity on its Old Ford site.

Both sectors could attract like new investment to the area. The West of England Development Agency is also looking to identify key sites in the region for new investment. Ideally, they should be over 40 acres. The only location in Mendip that meets this criteria is the Coalway Lane site in Frome.

It is perhaps premature to expect too much of the fledgling Regional Development Agency, or to hold out the prospect of a major international company moving to Frome. Such companies require locations in regional centres where they have access to large labour markets.

Nonetheless, with the first flush of initiatives in place to improve the town centre and its image within the region, one could be forgiven for being optimistic that we can really attract a clutch of new employers to Frome with the approach of the millennium.

CHAPTER 18

THE FROME
TOWN BAND

— Tony Brown —

The bard is often quoted for his 'music hath charms' etc. What would he have made of the sight of 200 young gentlemen of Round Table, dressed in dinner jackets, and at the end of what was supposed to have been a formal dinner, standing on their chairs, arms outstretched, each giving his own interpretation of a Lancaster bomber, turning and banking prior to landing?

All this under the influence of the Frome Town Band and an energetic rendering of 'The Dam Busters March', (with the help also, it has to be said, of a pint or two of the amber nectar).

Frome Town Band.

This is the scene repeated at different locations (and in different ways!) in Somerset and neighbouring counties recently and the Band's ability to cope with the extraordinary variety of jobs it is asked to do, is one of the reasons for its success.

Dinners, wedding receptions, church services of all kinds, fetes, carnival processions, concerts in theatres and churches, civic ceremonies of every kind, visits to Frome's twin towns of Chateau Gontier and Murrhardt, brass band contests, the list is endless and more varied than it has ever been in the 84 years of the Band's history.

Derived from the Army Volunteer Regimental Band of the 19th century, the military influence declined after the Second World War when woodwind instruments were abandoned, because of the difficulty of recruiting people to play them, and when ladies were welcomed into the Band. Both these changes, which were common to most brass bands, have been entirely beneficial.

The Frome Band has struggled over the years to remain independent and free of sponsorship. People in Frome speak of 'our Band' and their support and interest in the Band and its activities has been remarkable. The Supporters' Association, founded 20 years ago in order to free the Band of financial worry, has worked hard to do just that and has been able to present the Band Treasurer with substantial cheques each year.

In return, the playing members work hard at practices twice a week with at least one playing engagement in addition. The commitment in time and effort is considerable.

We are optimistic as to the future. Budget cuts in schools have not made it easier to recruit young musicians so we have founded a Junior Band and take every opportunity to interest young people in our activities. In this way we expect the people of Frome to have a town Band of which they can be proud for many years to come.

CHAPTER 19

FROME, A CARING TOWN

— John Moxon —

Most people like to think that their town is as caring a town as any other, but I would like to suggest that Frome is a step above most. What evidence is there for this?

For a town of its size, Frome's charitable institutions and endowments go back a long time. The Free Grammar School was founded in 1548, an almshouse for old women in 1461, the Blue School in 1728, and Keyford Asylum, a school for girls, in 1803. Many more charities were endowed over the years, and many exist today, or have been joined together for more practical purposes.

Twenty years ago, during what became known as 'The Winter of Discontent', we became concerned that some elderly or infirm people might suffer from the cold, during electricity or gas strikes. The Director of Social Services called together representatives of local active charitable organisations. We arranged to visit every home of a pensioner or infirm person and list what type of heating they had, and whether they had alternative heating or family help available.

We organised community halls with industrial paraffin heaters, throughout the town where people could stay and cooked meals would be provided. This all involved Rotary, Lions, Round Table, WRVS, Army Cadets, St. John's and Red Cross, etc, who offered their immediate help without hesitation. The Director told us that whenever he had a call for help, he hoped it was from the Frome area, because they had so many endowed charities and active charitable organisations. I am quite certain that should a problem on such a large scale arise again, Frome's many service organisations would quickly come forward and work together.

Frome's annual children's and adult Carnival procession collect ever increasing funds for the Carnival Charity. The Christmas Float consisting of a realistic Father Christmas in his sleigh drawn by two beautiful reindeer, manned by Rotary and Lions Club members working together, delights children and collects funds for ten evenings each December.

As well as very active service clubs: two Rotary, a Lions, Round Table, Rotaract, Frome has active RAFA, RNAssn, British Legion, a Day Centre, and every conceivable aid organisation. The popular 'Fun Run' efficiently organised each year by the Lions Club

A face change at Town Fete.

attracts people of many ages to join in, and many are sponsored for charity. How Frome cares about its appearance is well-demonstrated by its brilliant displays of flowers in beds and hanging baskets by its talented municipal gardeners, encouraraging others to join in the 'Frome in Bloom' competition, run for so long by much loved former teacher 'OPJ'. Local successes by business and amateurs in this competition have lead to the town's success in the regional and national competitions.

Other active local welfare organisations include Action Aid, Action on Disability, Adult Basic Learning, Age Concern, Alzheimer's Disease Support Group, Arthritis Care, Barnardo's Shop, Berkley Down Community Assn, BRCS, CLIC, Care Frome, Carers Group Frome, Chernobyl Children Nunney, CAB, Cruse, Frome College Caring and The Community, Frome Area Volunteers, Frome Family Centre, Gateway Club, Horticultural Therapy, Toy Library, Mencap, Meals on Wheels, Mendip Disability Information & Advocacy, Motor Neurone Disease Assn, Opportunity Playgroup, Oxfam shop, Positive Action on Cancer, Relate, Riding for the Disabled, Selwood Pony Driving School, SCA for the Blind, St John Ambulance, Talking Newspapers, WRVS, and Young people Frome.

There will be many I have missed out, for which I apologise, but this list is already huge for one medium-sized market town. The many youth organisations, church organisations and many other associations and clubs do charitable work, and lots of national charities have local representatives. We have a well-equipped Fire Brigade, Ambulance Service, our own Community Hospital with many visiting consultants, X-ray department, 24 hour casualty service, Maternity Unit, a large modern Health Centre with a 13 doctor partnership also manning a satellite surgery on the other side of town. Another medical partnership has its modern surgery premises, a further general practitioner is just starting up, and in the villages nearby first class practices also operate.

Frome has two veterinary practices, one very large, will be pleased to look after anything from your pet canary to your pet lion (if you live at Longleat!)

It is no fun to be in need of help, but I cannot think of a town more likely to provide that help gladly. Frome has a lot of caring people.

CHAPTER 20

CENTRE FOR TOURISTS

— Sheila Nicholson —

Frome is popularly used as a centre to stay whilst visiting the many tourist attractions which are within easy reach of it and its beautiful surrounding unspoilt countryside.

Only four miles away lies one of the nation's most visited historic houses, Longleat House, beautifully restored, with its priceless furnishings and collections, and the present Marquess's famous paintings. Its amazing Safari Park is as popular as ever, with its herds of buffalo, giraffe and zebra, its lions and many other species.

Equally popular amongst the nation's gardeners is the National Trust's Stourhead Gardens, of indescribable beauty all the year round. Other historic houses include Corsham Court, Bowood House, Montacute, Wilton and Stourhead House. Many historical monuments are also within easy reach, Avebury, Stonehenge, and castles Farleigh Hungerford, Wardour and Nunney, and the sites of Westbury White Horse and Cerne Abbas.

Museums to visit after Frome's own excellent one, with its authentic old chemist's shop, include Radstock's, reflecting its

Prizewinning conversion of old drying tower to Tourist Office.

Double header to thrill us all at David Shepherd's East Cranmore Railway.

mining past, Trowbridge reflecting its woollen heritage, Bath's Costume Museum and the authentic American Museum. Gardens at Iford and Hazelbury Manor join Longleat and Stourhead in providing popular summer concerts or plays. Beautiful Castle Combe, nearby, has regular motor racing meetings and driving courses.

Closer to Frome are some delightful attractions, Rode Bird Gardens has 1200 species of birds, Norwood Rare Breed Farm and David Shepherd's East Somerset Railway provide popular regular visits for the family.

Golf is available in Frome and several courses are nearby. Football, rugby, cricket, hockey have great support and many junior teams, the majorettes troupes are great competition winners, and Frome's renowned Town Band is supported by an excellent junior marching band.

We do not think many towns could better Frome for its interest and its surroundings.

CHAPTER 21

MARKET SUCCESS

— Alan Sandall —

Cries of horror echoed round our ancient town when the Somerset Standard broke the news that the livestock market was to move out of town. Just three miles away but it seemed the end of the world! It is on record that farmers have been doing business in the market town, and with its folk, since before the notable Domesday Book.

The success of that move in March 1990, and the way the town has been able to attract people to shop on Wednesdays – now there is room to move – has changed views immensely. No-one in the debate to keep the market in town could remember that the townspeople had clamoured in 1875 to move the congestion to what was then the edge of town, although then that was just a few hundred yards from the Market Place. What a difference that must have made.

It certainly has this time. Town and local government is working together, just as they did before, to make the old cattle market area into something worthy of more than just auctioneers' shouting. And, most importantly, the Livestock Market is the fastest-growing in the country and it has most certainly put Frome on the map.

When Cooper & Tanner, operators since 1883, was told by Mendip council the lease would not be renewed, the partners already knew in their hearts that if they did not move the market would die. There was no way the minute central market, built for the days of ponies and carts, could cope with the huge juggernaut lorries.

The die cast, led by Cooper & Tanner's senior partner David Millard, the chartered surveyors made a brave and momentous decision to move their roots. They bought a dairy farm beside the A36, at Standerwick, and built an agricultural centre on 30 acres.

This was something that had people in the whole farming world raising their eyebrows. Not just an acre-plus of covered penning, with three selling rings, but offices for their professional business, a carpeted restaurant and licensed bar, and a huge multi-purpose conference hall, easily divided in two.

The big Plus was parking for 350 cars and 40 huge lorries. Within months these areas, and the penning, had to be extended to cope with demand, especially as the bypass proved such a boon.

From that first opening sale on March 23, 1990, it has become a leading regional centre. "Through-put has grown beyond the wildest expectations", to quote the words of Mr Millard.

Total value of stock sold in the market is approaching £30 million a year! Buyers and farmers travel more that 100 miles to use it. There is an average each week of 250 beef cattle, 200 barren cows, 500 store cattle, 60 dairy, 500 calves, and 1,200 sheep.

Today a deal with Premier Livestock Auctions Ltd, of Yeovil, means PLA owns the livestock market area, with Cooper & Tanner still the auctioneers. Cooper & Tanner continue to own the professional services and keep their headquarters, plus the shops, offices, conference hall, restaurant and bar. The firm has also been able to return to estate agency business in Castle Cary and Glastonbury, as well as from the Agricultural Centre headquarters.

Aerial view of the new Frome Market.

With this neat arrangement with PLA, the agricultural centre continues to grow. Already Mole Valley Farmers has a thriving business on the site, and local agricultural engineers have built next door. Others will follow but new businesses must be agriculturally related.

Four years earlier the reality facing the C&T auctioneers was how to keep the warmth and friendliness which had been so important to the market for so long. It was vital that it had to be more than a livestock market, it had to be an agricultural centre.

There has to be a feeling of success. Cooper & Tanner's long and close relationship with Frome is strengthened, but not just on Wednesdays with the crowds around colourful market stalls, the shops, the produce market, and the 'deadstock' auction with all its gems.

It is the halls, with the food and drink facilities, being used all the time for conferences, farmers' gatherings, Young Farmers meetings, dinners, dances, weddings — and unique with its own Harvest Festival — have turned the agricultural centre into a much appreciated farming community centre-point. It even has a much-welcomed Bishop-appointed market chaplain.

CHAPTER 22

COMMUNITY EDUCATION

— *Malcolm Lloyd* —

Frome enjoys its Community Campus. Thousands of people use its facilities at the College every week, attending as full or part time students, using the Sports Centre, visiting the Merlin Theatre or joining one of the many clubs and societies that call the college 'home'. In many ways the facilities are unique, and the spirit that created and now maintains those facilities is equally special. Without that spirit the buildings would be just empty shells. The ideal of life-long learning is central to the college's philosophy and underpins all that the college strives to achieve.

The Community College is unique because the people of Frome have created it, supported it and made it grow. As an institution it never stands still. There is always a new project, another idea, another group of people pushing it forward. Recent growth has been tremendous, but its roots as a community college started early in the seventies.

As the new teaching blocks were being built to cope with the demands of the comprehensive school, the Merlin Theatre, Sports Centre and Youth wing were created. A red gras hockey pitch, soccer and softball leagues soon followed. Before long there was a parking problem as evening classes, theatre audiences, swimmers and badminton players competed for space.

Today the college boasts more recent work as, following the sale of the Park Road site, all activities located at Bath Road. A pottery and art room were built into the college art department for community use. The Community Education Centre was opened in 1992, and Littleoaks Day Nursery was built in 1993. Extra parking spaces, a refurbished Technology Department, computer suites and a Maths workshop show that the college is keeping up to date with community needs and the National Curriculum.

The link with Europe has never been stronger, epitomised by the magnificent European Community of Stones, opened in 1992. Built by local people and industry pulling together, the amphitheatre not only hosts an annual summer festival but provides a constant and wonderful reminder of the world beyond Frome.

Frome demands a lot from its college. The campus is alive from morning till night every day of the week. Students of all ages are offered a large variety of opportunities to further

Principal of Frome College, Mr Barry Bates with some of the 1995 college award winners.

their education and pursue leisure and recreational interests.

Training for the work place has never been more important, and this is reflected in the vocational courses which are offered, and in links with other agencies that ensure Frome and its people are well served for the future. The Community College has always promoted learning as a life-long process and has always believed in being part of its local community. As such, it is central to the town and surrounding area, and an essential part of life in Frome.

CHAPTER 23

UNIQUE CHURCHES
AND CHAPELS

— Rev. Ward Jones —

After years of decline the churches of Frome have begun to show signs of expansion and growth, as a visit to any of them on a Sunday morning will make clear. A number of individual congregations have increased both in size and the variety of their activities. And, compared to days gone by when there would have been a keen competitive edge between the denominations, the 1980s and 90s have seen a willingness to share in co-operative ventures, co-ordinated in recent years by Frome Area Churches' Together (F.A.C.T.)

Joint projects have included shared worship, study programmes, and chaplain (officially described as the churches' Schools Liaison Officer), David Russell, to serve the schools in the town. An expert in work with teenagers in particular, he has done much to put a 'human-face' on the Church for the youngsters of the town's 1500 strong tertiary Community College. In 1993 he achieved the distinction of being voted Most Popular Teacher of the Year!

Much could be written about the history of the various church buildings, but that information can be found elsewhere in a variety of other more detailed books and pamphlets. In the spirit of this book, in what follows, an attempt has been made to draw out and illustrate some of the more interesting features of a number of our town's main church buildings.

The Parish church of St. John the Baptist, parts of which dated back to the 12th century, is the oldest of Frome's ecclesiastical properties, having itself replaced a much more ancient foundation of St. Aldhelm. The Via Crucis and forecourt on to Bath Street are noteworthy, but its real claim to fame lies in its proud association with Bishop Thomas Ken.

Thomas Ken was Bishop of Bath and Wells, until deprived for refusing allegiance to William III while James II still lived. He died in 1711 and his grave is in the churchyard against the east wall of the church, covered by a later stone canopy. A chapel in the church, restored by the Marchioness of Bath in 1848 to his memory, contains many features relating to Ken, and the church possesses other precious relics of him. In 1961 a statue of Ken in episcopal robes was placed near the chapel to commemorate the 250th anniversary of his death.

Saint Mark.

It was the unpopularity of pew rents levied at St. Johns which led to the erection in 1818 of Christ Church, Frome. Built for the 'labouring poor' by way of public subscription, one of its earliest parishioners was the local philanthropist Thomas Bunn who lies buried in the churchyard. The recent 'self-help' transformation of the interior, now bright and welcoming, is a testimony to the dedication and commitment of ordinary caring parishioners.

Another interior transformation, more revolutionary in its consequences, has been that affected at Wesley Methodist Church. Here a traditional 800 seater, galleried non-Conformist Chapel was re-ordered in the mid 1980's to produce an upstairs 300 seater worship-centre with a suite of ancillary premises down below. One consequence of this project has been to highlight the organ.

The original one-manual instrument, reputed to have been bought second hand from Romsey Abbey in 1853 or 1854 has been both added to and rebuilt over the years. Perhaps the most noteworthy restoration involved a complete rebuilding in 1889, an event marked with recitals given by Sir Frederick Bridge, organist of Westminster Abbey, and Dr Alcock, organist at the Royal Albert Hall. Subsequent restoration and renovation work has followed to preserve this unique instrument.

One notable example of churches growing together in the twentieth century, against the pattern of division and dissent in previous centuries, is the United Reformed Church on Whittox Lane. In 1967 Zion and Rook Lane Congregational chapels joined to form today's church family.

The present building opened in 1810 – formerly Zion Congregational Church – is the successor to another property also known as Zion Chapel and originally home to a small Moravian congregation in the 18th century. The interior is appealing for its non-conformist plainness and order, typified by its box pews. Complete with their doors, numbers, namecard holders and umbrella holders they testify to a previous age when people paid pew rents and woe-betide anyone who sat in 'your' pew. Until a recent reordering of part of the premises a letterbox was set into one of the original walls, through which people could post their pew rents.

Undoubtedly the chief treasure of the Anglican Holy Trinity Church (opened in 1838 and built in an Early English Gothic Style) is the collection of beautiful stained glass windows by Morris and Co. from designs by Burne Jones. The dedications are worth studying. There is only space to consider one of the group:

St. Mark – Erected at the Dedication Festival 1894, the gift of Mr Horatio Channon, for many years a worshipper in the Church.

Also there is the large window over the entrance, depicting St. John the Baptist, St. Paul and St. Katherine was the gift of Harry Hams, the Blue Coat Boy who became a trustee and benefactor of the Frome Charities, and died 1887. Erected 1903.

The window above the Altar was given in memory of the first Vicar in 1876.

The Catholic community in Frome enjoys the distinction of being part of the oldest denomination, while worshipping in the most recent and only modern ecclesiastical building in the town. The Church of St. Catharine, in Park Road, was opened in

Aerial view shows Frome's mediaeval streets survive.

Acknowledgement: Philip Waite Photography

1968 (being extended in the 1990s), replacing what is now the church hall. The hall, itself used for worship since 1928, had replaced a building off Whittox Lane which had been in use since the mid-nineteenth century.

Other churches in the town include St. Marys (linked with St. Johns), Portway Methodist, Sheppard's Barton Baptist, the Congregational Church, the Society of Friends, and Selwood Community Church. Together with those mentioned in greater detail, they all look forward confidently to serving the population of Frome in the new millennium – working together and sharing their diversity to the Glory of God.

CHAPTER 24

POLICING SMALL TOWNS

— Inspector Steve Gazzard —

The nature and amount of crime has changed in the small towns in the West Country over the past decade or so. This is partly due to the changes in the life style of the population; it has become more mobile, with more cars per household, more fast roads for criminals to make their rapid departure, holiday habits causing more empty houses, and increasing long-term unemployment in a more materialistic world causing an increase in thieving.

The good news, is that the quality and effectiveness of the Police Force has changed too, and more than meets this increase in crime, though you might be surprised to learn this, if you take your information from the newspapers. The substantial reorganisation of the Avon and Somerset Police which took place in 1992, changed the Frome Station from covering a large sub-division with a Superintendent, Chief Inspector, three Inspectors, and eight sergeants, to housing a local force under myself, an Inspector, as Frome Commander.

The large increase in crime, and reduced finances available to fight it, which caused the reorganisation, lead to a streamlining which has resulted in crime being dealt with very adequately. Red tape has been vastly reduced, and decisions can be taken on the spot to deal with whatever problem has arisen, causing the local force to be fast and flexible. Inevitably, there has been some targeting of these reduced resources, and this has been towards violence, burglary, and car-related offences.

We have had excellent support from the public, particularly groups such as Neighbourhood Watch, the Crime Prevention Panel, Special Constables, Police and Community Consultative Groups, Licensed Victuallers Association and Chamber of Commerce, with support of the Town and District Councils. Our intelligence system is at its highest level ever, under our Crime Management Unit, with high level technology, and we have excellent mobility in well-maintained vehicles. We can call on our neighbouring forces for rapid assistance, if necessary, as well as the Task Force.

Frome's reported crime is at its lowest level in the 12 years I have been here, and our detection rate is up. We have the highest arrest per officer, putting us head and shoulders above any other Section similarly staffed. There is still room for improvement, and much

Good relations between Police and Public are vital to fight crime.

of this will come when our customers, the public, accept the need to become even more crime conscious. They must remember 'lock it or lose it' applies to their houses as well as cars and bikes.

We can be very proud of our achievement and our logo 'Working for you, working with you', and I am confident that with our increasing use of technology, mobility and fast response, and the public's increasing awareness and co-operation, the people of Frome may look forward to its remaining top of the league in the Yeovil District, with a reduction of crime and increase in its detection.

At a time when the increasing crime rate is a constant topic of conversation, always in the news media and much-discussed by our politicians, am glad to be able to tell Frome's townspeople this good news.

CRIME PREVENTION

— Alan Sandall —

There is strong support for the Police among the community. One thousand Neighbourhood Watch groups operate in the town and surrounding villages. Each has its own co-ordinator and works closely with the Police community liaison officer.

This is typical of the support given by local people when action is needed. Making them really valuable is a new computer-controlled warning system which enables Watch members to be alerted quickly and simply.

Utilising the technology, co-ordinators are told of more serious crime in their area. House burglaries, violent crimes where witnesses are sought, and deceptions involving the vulnerable, for examples. It provides detailed information, how and where, special security warnings, and a call to be on the lookout.

Messages about possible problem people, their transport, or repetitive crimes, for example, are dictated into the computer which then automatically telephones Neighbourhood Watch co-ordinators spreading the knowledge with great speed.

Also active is a Crime Prevention Panel formed early in 1995. This brings together a wealth of knowledge and experiences to stimulate actions to widen public awareness of the traits and trends of 'villains'.

Already a pilot scheme is going ahead to involve schoolchildren in a Family Security Pledge. Working with their grown-ups, they will study both home and car security, and, hopefully, be more aware of their personal safety. At the other extreme, doorstickers are being produced to remind the elderly, 'Don't be conned!' into letting people into their homes. There is also a Police Consultative Group to ensure good relations are maintained.

All this means, as Inspector Gazzard's article emphasises, that Frome is facing up to and is well placed in the battle against a national problem.

CHAPTER 25

CATHERINE HILL

— Julie Grail —

The plight of retailing is constantly changing. Gone are the days of the 'butcher, baker and candlestick maker' selling to the familiar customer, operating a half day and lunchtime closing, and living above the shop. Changes in lifestyles are considerably affecting the way in which we shop, and more importantly the times of day and the days of the week.

Convenience is increasingly the most influential element in deciding where one shops, particularly for the weekly groceries. With the increasing amounts of car-borne shoppers this is further enforced, particularly by the desire to park close by and free of charge. This aspect of the retailing game is increasingly being won by the large supermarket chains especially those on edge/out of town sites.

Durable and DIY goods are also moving out of town centres to benefit from advantages of greenfield sites and to, again, offer that important convenience factor. Further displacement from the town centres is threatened by the potential of 'teleshopping' which allows purchasing of goods and services with just a mere touch of a button on your home computer.

So what does all this mean for the town centre of a small market town such as Frome, and for a run-down area such as Catherine Hill? It means an opportunity to specialise – to differentiate from the modern convenience style development of the 1980s and 1990s, and to build on the historical and architectural qualities that Frome boasts. This means offering a unique shopping experience of interest both to local people and tourists alike by seeking to complement the 'essential' shopping with aspects of specialist retailing.

This style of shopping is rapidly becoming a pastime in itself. Catherine Hill lends itself well to this area. It was traditionally one of the main shopping streets in Frome, however in recent times the vitality of the area has diminished due to the changes in retailing. To the extent that in January, 1995, 60% of the properties stood vacant and were in a poor state of repair.

Drawing on its character as an attractive historic street it was deemed worthy of revitalisation. Catherine Hill lies south west of the Market Place. Its name originates from the medieval chantry chapel of St Katherine which was in the area. The chapel was in

Catherine Street Fair.

existence as early as c 1279 and it is thought was located on the site of the present 14 and 15 Catherine Hill. Number 13 shows evidence of medieval origin, and appears to have been gutted in the mid 16th century, probably due to the dissolution of the chantry in 1548.

Buildings on the south side of the hill suggests a late 17th century origin and traditionally belonged to the Champneys family of Orchardleigh. Many additions have been made since that time, the majority being in the late 19th century.

Plans for the revitalisation of Catherine Hill began in late 1994 with the establishment of a small working party. In January of 1995, when an officer was appointed by Mendip District Council to deal with the town centre, the project formally came into being. An important first step was to establish a clear picture of the current situation and to consider the future potential of the area. An array of possible options was considered ranging from a 'do nothing' to a 'themed tourist attraction'.

Drawing on the recommendations of the Civic Trust study 1, it was identified Frome benefited from a particular talent in arts and crafts that was largely concealed at the present time. Taking into account the move of the focus of retailing in the town, it was also felt necessary to consider specialist types of retailing that would not rely purely on passing trade.

Putting this into the context of retailing nationally, and locally the rest of Frome, it was decided that the preferred option for the revitalisation would be 'specialist retailing, particularly in arts, crafts and antiques, and appealing to the wider tourist trade'.

However, having established this strategy, there was still a need to consider the longer term trends. With 60% vacancy rates in the Hill, further vacancies the length of Catherine Hill and Street in the longer term was unrealistic, hence an opportunity to convert properties back to residential use was required. The planning policy was amended in order to facilitate this and therefore to establish a 'critical mass' of retailing at the bottom end. Hence offering a more flexible approach to potential investors.

When considering the strategy in detail, it was felt an important factor of the demise of the area, and subsequent revitalisation, had been the disproportionately high Business Rates. This was dealt with by firstly inviting the District Valuer to the Task Force to present a paper on the issue. Discussions followed and the result was a blanket reduction of Rateable Values by approximately 20-30%. This greatly helped the confidence in the area.

Due to the length of time the properties had stood vacant the majority were in a poor state of repair. Although all the private landlords were willing to reduce rents and offer negotiable terms, potential traders still required a further incentive. In response a retail grant was set up by Mendip District Council on a pilot basis of one year. The grant is of a matched funding nature and is intended to help fund capital start up costs of setting up business on the Hill.

The strategy for the revitalisation is now well underway and vacancy rates are falling. The intention was to create a specialist retailing area which developed a specific niche and hence its own reputation. The progress to date is proving the project successful with the vacancy rate already reduced to 30%.

The types of shops being attracted are those within the arts, crafts and antique sectors, as desired. Antiques and collectible are developing well, others include a wood-turner, clock maker/repairer, and a handpainted-furniture shop. The plan is to develop an active area of specialist retailing which is more than just a street of shops. Craft workshops on site demonstrating how their products are made, helps to create a wider shopping experience, particularly as a tourist attraction.

Tourists are naturally attracted to Catherine Hill and start walking up it, and will be pleased to continue up on finding more shops in use. It is hoped that more people would be directed to exploring Catherine Hill if plans for Rook Lane Chapel materialise. It is hoped that visitors, on leaving the chapel, will be encouraged to explore Frome via Catherine Hill.

The chapel itself, recently renovated, is now owned by Mendip District Council, and plans for the future of this impressive Grade I listed building, built in 1707, are underway. The proposal is a National Puzzle Museum and Interactive Puzzle Centre by an internationally renowned metagrobologist, James Dalgety.

The only permanent exhibitions of puzzles in the British Isles is James Dalgety's Puzzlequest in Cardiff which contain large interactive puzzles. The only permanent Museum of Puzzles in the World, is in the mountain town of Hikimi in Japan - nearly all of its antique exhibits were provided by James. The proposed puzzle centre will combine features from both into a unique and popular attraction.

James Dalgety has one of the world's best collections of antique puzzles, and he is the designer of many large interactive puzzles which are being used in museums and science centres all around the world. The collections range from coins engraved with labyrinths, from 320 BC, to prototypes of next years' plastic puzzles; from a huge 17th century Indian treasury chest to Chippendale tea caddies with secret compartments. They range from crudely made plastic roly-poly puzzles out of Christmas crackers to intricate pieces of puzzle jewellery and from children's riddles to Hieroglyphic Bibles.

Rook Lane Chapel, with its proposed extensions is an ideal building for the venture. It has tremendous presence and the internal spaces both of the chapel and its new extension could house a vibrant puzzle centre. From the town's point of view the Puzzle Centre would provide an internationally unique tourist attraction which could considerably improve the viability of the town.

Drawing to a close, where does this initiative put Frome in the future of retailing? In the age of 'one stop shopping' and 'push button purchases', in order to survive a town must diversify. It must be able to appeal to its customers within a wider sphere. Town centres of the future must develop into vital and viable places to live, work and play. Catherine Hill has an opportunity to develop such a specialist area to give Frome the prosperous future it deserves. The evidence to date looks promising, long may it continue.

Note:

1. The Civic Trust report 'Frome Town Centre. An Environmental Audit' (1995) was commissioned by Mendip District Council and part funded by English Heritage. It represents a comprehensive study of the town centre of Frome and its potential for the future.

CHAPTER 26

ARTS AND CRAFTS

— *John Moxon* —

Frome has more artists per head of population than most towns (one guess was over 500 resident artists) the excellent Civic Trust report on Frome quotes. Like them, one wonders if this is a bit over the top, but certainly Frome is producing, or has settled in it a considerable number of artists and craftsmen numbering amongst them some of outstanding talent. Exhibitions are frequent.

The outstanding evidence of Frome's commitment to the arts is the Black Swan Guild, Somerset's leading showcase of contemporary Arts and Crafts. It is a registered charity, set up in 1986 to promote a high standard of art and craft throughout the region, to draw on and contribute to the continuing tradition of fine art and crafts in Somerset. It is recognised as a unique and significant regional centre for the arts. It promotes artistic quality and originality, encouraging and exhibiting two and three-dimensional work of an innovative and challenging nature, produced by practising professional artists.

The Guild's fine public Gallery is one of the largest exhibition spaces in the county and has a constantly changing programme, including works of local artists as well as those of national and international renown. The Black Swan Guild also has its own battery of studios and workshops where artists can be seen working. There is also a very popular Wholefood Cafe and a Craftshop

Mediaeval plotters at St Catherine's Fair.

Young Mozart charms Bath in their Parade Gardens.

Sculpted by David Backhouse of Frome.

displaying high quality work permanently, with also short individual exhibitions. The Guild also holds classes and day schools, and organises schools visits and resources for education. It is joining with Mendip District Council in promoting the setting up of individual craft shops in Catherine Hill.

Frome has other opportunities of seeing major exhibitions of art in the large professional gallery in the Studio Prints shop in the precinct. This has staged the largest ever exhibition of David Shepherd's paintings, covering a huge variety of subjects. The Merlin Theatre also mounts regular exhibitions in its gallery, and the quality of the work of the students in the large art department of Frome Community College is well worth seeing at their exhibitions.

Frome Art Society is active with over one hundred members of all ages and abilities. Lectures and demonstrations are held monthly during the winter months at Frome Community College. Twice a year exhibitions of members' work are held at The Black Swan Gallery.

Embroiders' Guilds Frome and District Branch has an amazing thirty two members, outgrowing the room allocated to it and erecting their own. They meet regularly, with workshops and visiting lecturers, and exhibit their beautiful work around the country. Frome Quilters have been growing over the past five years and enjoy sharing their skills and talents. The Frome Photographic Society meet regularly and their talents are to be seen amongst the photographs in this book. The Frome and District Writers Circle meet monthly, as does The Sugar Craft Club, and two Flower Arranging Societies. The Frome

Horticultural Society meets monthly and has its own high standard show.

Amongst individual artists and craftsmen in the area Christopher Barlow's 'Early Keyboard' instruments and harps are outstanding. Based on antique models found in museums and collections, they are often used for 'authentic' performances of the Baroque composers. Christopher's harpsichords can sometimes be heard with performances by some of the local choirs and other music groups, including events at the Great Elm Music Festival. Nigel Kennedy (yes!) used a large double manual harpsichord of Christopher's for a recent recording. Christopher's spinets, clavichords, harpsichords

Superb marquetry by Christopher Vickers.

often have beautiful paintings of flowers and birds on their soundboards painted by his mother, who lives in Frome. At the time of writing Christopher is building a fortepiano based on one that Mozart played. He also does valuable restoration work, especially on antique pianos.

Christopher Vickers concentrates on making exquisite boxes, including jewellery and sewing boxes with inlaid lids, featuring fine hard cut dovetail joints and removable trays. He uses native box, oak, laburnum, yew and walnut burrs. He also makes wall mirrors, inlaid with contrasting woods, stained glass or enamels, and a selection of clocks.

David Backhouse attended nearby Warminster School, trained in Bristol and lives in one of Frome's surrounding villages. His fame as a sculptor is international, and Frome people were delighted when Sainsbury's commissioned him to sculpt for their new store, a bas relief using local children as models. His many busts include those of the Marquess of Bath, Jose Carreras and Dame Alicia Markova, and he has held one-man exhibitions in London, New York and Washington, and his sculpture may be found in the City of London, Bristol City Centre, Holland Park, and Bath amongst many other places.

Frome has an outstanding potter, in Russell Coates, who learned his art and taught at Goldsmiths College, but has been much influenced by Professor Fujio Kitade during three years in Japan and uses the traditional old Kutani colours of red, yellow, green, blue and purple on his porcelain decoration of Japanese or Celtic design.

This beautiful kingfisher and the exquisite bowl are by Frome's talented Russell Coates.

Amongst other local potters, Philip Wood's popular ceramics are to be found at his gallery in Nunney. One of Frome's oldest sculptors and artists is probably Charles Hopkins, who was still teaching A level students until nearly eighty. He worked in many different media, including stone, metal, and fibreglass. His work is often found in schools, including the lamb to be seen over the portal of St John's School. He also has a peacock, worked in metal, in Wells Cathedral.

Frome is full of musical talent. The prize-winning Frome Town Band is in great demand, its Youth Orchestra and Youth Choir are well-supported. Frome has a Choral Society as well as an Operatic Society who have produced ambitious shows for more than sixty years. Frome's Dramatic Society is a frequent winner at the two-day Maria Ritchie Festival of one act plays. Frome College, Selwood and Oakfield Middle Schools now use the Ecos outdoor amphitheatre to perform their shows to a wider public.

I am indebted to Isobel George who has taught and helped so many, for her help in providing me with information for this article.

CHAPTER 27

MANY CHOICES FOR YOUTH

— Alan Sandall —

Looking forward often involves starting looking back - and getting surprises. No one in the local Scouting Movement knew that Scouting began in Frome only two years after it was 'invented' by Baden-Powell in 1908! Frome was quick to take the lead, as usual.

Frome's young people 85 years ago quickly found activities to excite them, as they can today. Guiding and Scouting are both still big attractions, but there are now many varied alternatives. The smart 'military' units are the Air Training Corps and the Army Cadets, which has its own Somerset's quick step band. There are the St John's Ambulance Cadets and those of the British Red Cross, whose successful junior marching band has now become independent.

Many take part in lively sporting action; Rugby especially, with well over two hundred players involved in age groups from seven to eighteen years, as well as the senior teams, on the modern Gypsy Lane sports complex. The Club also has an all ladies XV.

The amazing list of sports Frome people play is included in Bob Beacham's article 'Frome at Play', and all these encourage juniors, some very actively. They are also welcomed for action in a a wide field from conservation, dance, drama, majorettes – hugely successful in Frome – to the Duke of Edinburgh's Award Scheme. An overwhelming stream of activities – no one who has tried, could possibly be bored!

Frome is a very musical town, with its Choral Society and 'Operatic', its Music Society and Town Band, so one is not surprised to find there is a strong Youth Choir and Youth Orchestra. The Rotary Club has contributed too, by founding the Rotaract Club, a service club for both sexes from 18 to 30. They manage to intersperse significantly helping the local and international community with having a whale of a good time, and can often be seen at a 'Children in need' gathering on TV in outrageous garb.

In the 50 years the Frome Youth and Community Centre has been running, Richard Watson tells me "many things have changed and things have moved on from the days of ballroom dancing and rifle shooting; the building is more in use than at any time in its life." He describes what a wide cover of service the centre seeks to provide, including initiating

Frome Rugby Club's much envied clubhouse is seen in the background. The club is proud that it has as many members as mighty Bath.

discussion groups, a social meeting place for young people leaving care, and the provision of a facility which allows young people to practice playing music. He is one of the team of youth workers centred there and elsewhere in the community who go out to meet people in their own environments.

The centre is also the home of the district youth work team which supports youth work groups all over the area. The Vallis Road Centre is also the home of a great variety of community-user groups, the ghastly modern jargon for such things as badminton clubs, volleyball and model car racing! It is also used by Social Services for day care, and by the Vallis Playgroup.

"Staff are available to meet with young people and discuss their ideas," Richard said, "we welcome the opinions of young people on the programme and the work we do. We hope they will become actively involved in the wider community as a result of their contact with us."

I briefly mentioned Scouting at the beginning, and finish by mentioning how they have moved with the times too, and what they have to offer young people of this modern age. Young people between six and 20 are offered a variety of pursuits; caving, climbing, sailing, and camping are but a taste of their 'adventures'. "The young people are still encouraged to do their 'good turn' but in a different way to that foreseen by the founder of Scouting, Robert Baden-Powell, the hero of the siege of Mafeking," said District Commissioner Keith Bayliss.

Frome Scouts have their own site at nearby Tedbury, and open it to troops and packs countrywide. Many young boys and girls know Frome because of holidaying under canvas at Tedbury. To answer those who sit about in bored groups saying there is nothing to do and answer suggestions by saying they cannot afford to join activities, just an idea of some comparable costs might help. The county Youth Service charges about 30p per session, trips and other activities are subsidised, so not expensive. Scouting, about £1 per week, plus cost of uniform, often second hand, a few pounds, with a little for extra activities such as sailing.

As so often, it is all a matter of choices. No town has more activities to offer its young people, and most of them gladly take an active part in them. Far from being complacent, however, more facilities are being sought and planned, young people are the future and Frome clearly realises this.

CHAPTER 8

FROME CHEESE SHOW

— Dennis Pattinson —

Frome Cheese Show, so named from the earlier fairs in the town when cheese was the major exhibit among the many products for sale, has long played a part in the life of the area. The present show is believed to be descended from fairs recorded in Frome in 1785, and itself dates from 1861.

Like the major fairs, the Cheese Fair was pitched in the Market Place, Bath Street and the surrounding streets. Hundreds of tons of cheese changed hands, Frome being the largest of all the cheese fairs, and cheese came from far and wide to be sold here. In 1874 the Market

Superior cheeses are still to be found at Frome Cheese Show.

Hall was built by local farmers to improve matters for both buyers and sellers and around that time the Frome and District Agricultural Society was formed to encourage farmers to compete in various improving ideas and systems.

The show as it became, with its many classes for competitors and exhibitors, was held in the Market Hall and the old Cattle Market Yard and soon expanded across the river into what is now part of Singers Factory. A bridge of large baulks of timber was erected across the river for each Show, and on one occasion when it collapsed animals and people fell into the water.

The Show Committee decided it was time to look for a better venue for the event. The Cricket Ground was bought in 1921, and later, the whole of the present Showground of 32 acres. This is now leased to Mendip District Council, but they have to quit the area for the period of the Show.

Growth of interest has widened classes held, which of course, include cheese of many varieties, but still mainly Cheddar. Also there is butter, eggs, poultry, and British and Continental breeds of dairy and beef cattle. Horses including Hunters, Heavy horses and ponies, Showjumping and Carriage driving classes. Hundreds of dogs compete in the Dog Show, which is not far on the Showground from the Sheep and Goat competitors.

This splendidly restored wagon drawn by shire horse, at Frome Cheese Show.

The Grain and Fodder section caters for the agrarian interest, horticulturists and flower arrangers compete in the flower tent, whilst all are in awe of the Floral trade stands. In the Handicraft tent mothers compete with daughters, aunts (and the occasional somebody's husband) in the homecraft sections, whilst the quality of exhibits among the classes of needlework, of art, or photography are of a quite exceptional standard. There is also a tent which is the animal nursery where youngsters of all ages can see and stroke, and chat about the young of all sorts of animals.

Around the avenue there are craft stalls and rare breeds, stands for combines and cars or crockery, stands for gardeners or graziers, for households or husbandmen, for plants or provender, stalls where you can buy a piece of the past or pay for a part of your future – and people galore. The Marquess of Bath was there as President in this year of 1995, along with many of his fellow Patrons. There will be tiny babies being introduced by proud parents with 'Yes, it's his first show', and old friends being helped around. Helpers and Stewards, paid or unpaid, young and old, with nearby show committee members, are all dedicated to helping everyone enjoy a lovely day out. Frome Show is usually blessed by fine weather on the day. (The last wet show days both had a Beckington President on the day – Beckington, what had you done!?)

Birds and Beasts, Flowers and Friendship, Men and Machines are all to be seen, and may be examined, handled, refurbished or replaced. The Show tries to have something for everybody and may not please everyone but all should recognise that throughout its long history the Show has moved with the changing times.

The Show has now reverted to the third Wednesday in September and looks forward from a successful past and a fascinating present to an engaging future. The town is once again home to the largest cheese factors in Britain – long may its name be carried by one of Britain's foremost One Day Shows.

CHAPTER 29

A CROWN OF
STATELY HOMES

— Michael McGarvie —

The surroundings of Frome are rich in mansions despite the early loss of Witham House with its notable open portico and of Mells Park, burnt down in 1917. By far the grandest and most famous of these is Longleat. This was largely completed by 1580. On the surface the design was revolutionary with uniform facades which were symmetrical and ornamented with bays and classical detailing. Yet in its array of glass, position of the Great Hall and staircase, its courtyards and rooftop turrets, Longleat still contained traditional mediaeval forms. Sir John Thynne, the genius of the place, was secretary to the Lord Protector, the Duke of Somerset. In his portraits he looks a bruiser and, indeed, he was a bully and greedy for land and money. But his love of architecture was genuine, while after a campaign in Scotland he brought back as his booty a small collection of books which formed the nucleus of Longleat's library, the outstanding feature of the house.

Generations of Thynnes since Sir John's time have altered Longleat and inside little of his work survives. Among those whom he employed was a local man, William Spicer, from Nunney. He rose to become Surveyor of the Queen's Works. The interior is now dominated by the taste of the fourth Marquess of Bath who in the later 19th century transformed Longleat into a sumptuous Venetian palace, all gilt, flock and mural paintings. Outside, thanks to Capability Brown, the box-like structure of the house stands in a desert of lawn, the formal gardens which complemented it having been swept away due to changing fashion in the 1750s.

Sir John Thynne's master acquired the Maiden Bradley estate in 1538 and the house there is still the home of his descendant, the 19th Duke of Somerset, England's premier duke. The dignified but unexceptional building which stands today is only a fragment of the enormous mansion erected by Sir Edward Seymour, Speaker of the House of Commons, in the 1680s. His grandiose monument by Rysbrack is in the church. At that time the dukedom was vested in a younger branch of the family while Sir Edward was head of the senior line. When William III asked him if he were of the Duke of Somerset's family, he replied sharply that the duke was of his family. His handsome velvet saddle is still preserved in the house which was probably built for him by the Hurlbutts, Warwickshire carpenters.

Ancient Mells Manor.

In the 18th century, this branch of the Seymours inherited the dukedom and bought other great houses. Maiden Bradley was less frequented and eventually, in 1821, largely pulled down. What remained, said to be an eighth of the original structure, was used as a hunting box. Even this was neglected and had to be refurbished in the 1880s. The 15th duke made additions after his accession in 1894. While not overwhelmingly imposing, Bradley House is a practical proposition for a ducal family in the late 20th century, allowing an elegant setting without lions or other public attractions.

Bradley House was roofed, in part at least, with stone tiles from Marston Bigot, whose manor house has in recent years risen from the ashes. Marston House may have been designed by Robert Smythson, who worked at Longleat and who became the architect of Wollaton, near Nottingham, and of Hardwick Hall, Derbyshire. The plan of Marston with

Study of Marston House before spoiled by wartime occupation. It is now splendidly restored.

extruded corners has similarities with other Smythson buildings. The core of the original house of c 1600 remains amid the extensive pile created by the Boyle family, Earls of Cork and Orrery, who owned Marston from 1641 until 1905. The wings, remarkably Irish in feeling, were the work of Samuel Wyatt in 1776. The house was turned back to front in 1856 when Major C.E. Davis, the Bath City Architect, added the great entrance hall with its double cantilever staircase and fine arcades, as well as the ballroom and conservatory. After years of neglect and damage by military occupation, Marston House, verging on ruin, was bought by Foster Yeoman Ltd., a local quarry company, in 1984. Both John

Manor /
Roche '44

Yeoman, the chairman, and his wife Angela loved the house. They began a long and painstaking restoration with a view to turning the house into their company headquarters.

After John Yeoman's death in 1987, Mrs Yeoman carried on the good work which was substantially completed in 1990. The builders involved were Butchers of Warminster who converted the mansion to offices with outstanding skill and sensitivity. Traditional methods and materials were used. Marston House, once described as 'a pearl in an emerald setting', has regained its lustre and, as Mrs Yeoman makes the beautifully restored state rooms available for a variety of functions, also its place in the local community. Quarrying is much criticised, but the salvation of Marston is an example of the tangible benefits which can accrue from it.

In 1972, Marston House was threatened with demolition. Among those willing to see it go was Arthur Duckworth, of Orchardleigh. His vast house has been empty for nearly 10 years and its future is uncertain at the time of writing. Orchardleigh House is the most recent of our local mansions having been completed only in 1858. Its builder was William Duckworth, a Lancastrian lawyer, who employed Thomas Henry Wyatt, known amongst other attributes, as a designer of lunatic asylums, to plan what was intended to be a cheerful and comfortable home rather that 'a highly ornamental and pretentious building'. Wyatt came up with a neo-Elizabethan design on to which were grafted French renaissance elements, but producing a peculiarly 'gothick' effect.

The new house replaced the mediaeval manor of the Champneys in the valley below, a position so damp that frogs were said to serenade the drawing-room windows. This house was taken down in 1860. Today the glory of Orchardleigh is the park and the glory of the house is its superb site looking across the lake to the Down. Architecturally speaking, the house is uninspiring despite its saddle-back tower and tourelles. Inside, everything is of the best quality from its fire-proof frame to its fittings of sandalwood and birds-eye maple but this does not compensate for the dull halls and poor staircase. Perhaps the most interesting feature of the interior is the variety of styles used for its many fireplaces.

If Orchardleigh is a comparative newcomer among the stately homes of Frome, the Manor House of Mells is among the most ancient. In its exceptionally happy relationship with St. Andrew's Church, it creates a quintessential English scene of rare harmony and beauty. The manor house retains vestiges of the mediaeval residence of the Abbots of Glastonbury which John Leland, the king's antiquary, saw in 1540 close to the western end of the church. The abbot's walled garden with its distinctive buttresses remains.

The manor was bought by Thomas and John Horner for £1431 19s 11¾ d in 1543 from Henry VIII and His Majesty's grant and receipt hangs on the dining room wall to this day.

Some additions were made to the house in the 16th century and in the early 1600s it evolved into an H-shaped building grouped around two courtyards, that 'fair large house of stone' which the cavalier captain, Richard Symonds, described in 1644 when Charles I stayed there. The courtyards were each side of a classical porch which linked long north and south wings. In 1725, the Horners built a new mansion in the park and the old manor was partially demolished; the remainder became a farm-house. After a period as an ecclesiastical college, the manor house was restored from 1900 by Sir John Horner and his talented wife, Frances, and became the main residence of the family, now represented by Sir John's grandson, the Earl of Oxford and Asquith.

Lord Oxford's nephew is Lord Hylton whose house at Ammerdown is one of solid classical dignity well set in the landscape. It was built between 1788 and 1795 by Thomas Samuel Jolliffe, who had married an heiress of the Kilmersdon Twyfords. The architect was James Wyatt. The house was a small, cube-shaped villa whose walls were enlivened with pilasters and Venetian windows set in arched recesses. Manners and Gill, Bath architects, enlarged the house sympathetically in 1857. It contains a notable Chinese Hall and handsome domed staircase. The walled park which surrounds Ammerdown is four miles in circumference. It contains the well-known column which records how Mr Jolliffe reclaimed these wild lands and 'clothed them with fertility and verdure and embellished them with tasteful and ornamental decorations'. A more modern feature is the yew garden designed by Sir Edwin Lutyens in 1901 and not unlike his work at Mells Park.

Left: Longleat House.

CHAPTER 30

THE MEDIA ARE ALERT AND ALIVE

— Alan Sandall —

I wonder what the town's residents of the mid 19th century studying the first journal would say if they could compare with today - that is assuming they could afford, in 1854, to buy one.

It was aptly named The Sentinel, printed and published monthly by Mr Butler, of Butler & Tanner fame. He could not have foreseen the success of his printing company, spreading the name of Frome as a centre for printing excellence across the world.

The longest serving of the media is the Somerset Standard. Like other West Country newspapers it took a long time to shake off the shackles of traditional hot-metal production.

Local reporter Caroline Wood uses her word processor to send the news to the production centre in Bath. There with other companion newspapers of the Westminster Press division, Media in Wessex, her words, and those of all the other contributors, are changed immediately into columns of photographic paper to be made into its pages.

Days when the Standard could be printed in the former Ellenbray's shop, at the back of St John's Church, are long gone. The Editor Earl Moorhouse, my successor, has a much larger patch to watch over; not only the sister paper, the Guardian, serving Radstock and Midsomer Norton, but the Wells Journal and others serving Shepton Mallet and the Cheddar area.

The Western Daily Press a regional newspaper still owned locally by Bristol United Press focuses brightly on events as they happen. Its sister, the Bristol Evening Post, and the Standard's, Bath Chronicle, both make a contribution.

Free newspapers and magazines come and go. Today there is the Frome Star, from Media in Wessex, and the latest, the FosseWay, produced by Blackmore Vale Publishing Co.

Cable television, bringing competition to the discs of the pay-satellite system, will be arriving by 1997, as part of the massive area operation by United Artists.

Sixty years ago saw the beginnings of regional broadcasting from Bristol. All that time the BBC has been operating from Whiteladies Road. Many of its successes have become part of the national networks of TV as well as radio.

There are three Corporation programme-making operations in the city; the network production centre, which includes the brilliant natural history unit; the BBC West television; and Radio Bristol.

Creating this wide variety, the network centre produces hundreds of hours of top-class programmes a year, mainly for Radio 4, as well as fascinating TV. 'Any Questions?' became an early national institution, for example.

Radio Bristol has just celebrated its 25th birthday. It was the first of the new local broadcasting vision. By tradition it serves Frome, mainly from its Bath studio.

It's sister station Somerset Sound is one of the first in the country to be a digitised station. It can also be received in the Frome area and opts out of the main Bristol programme at various times of the day. From its own studios in Taunton and Bristol, it produces a separate early morning show, and news and information programmes, during the day and evening.

More and more the BBC reporters are bi-media trained. Reporters switch from being voices to people as they double to bring the news to the local television stations.

GWR is another local success story. It is the second largest radio group in the country. It began in 1982 as Wiltshire Radio and after a few years combined with Radio West in Bristol taking its present day name.

Over the next 10 to 15 years it grew, taking in stations at Reading, Bournemouth, and part shares in Devon and several others in the South. In 1993/94 it included first the Midland radio network and then another in Anglia.

Today as GWR FM, with Brunel Classic Gold, it aims to be the premier station. So does Radio Bristol, so listeners benefit from good, sound, professional competition.

Creeping in also is Radio Orchard, another commercial from Taunton, and Wiltshire Sound, also part of the Radio Bristol set-up, which takes a marginal interest.

Regularly during the day HTV, the financially successful Bristol and Wales commercial television group, present news programmes. HTV is also making a name with other programmes, building itself into a national and international business, with a record of achieving peak time successes to a range of channels.

It is in the area of 'new media' that the company has made the biggest strides recently, becoming one of the largest providers of programming to cable and satellite in the country.

HTV has during the year forged new national and international alliances, which spells good news for the future. From its studios it produces over 3,000 hours of programming annually, including 1,600 of cable television. It also scores well with natural history programmes made by its Partridge Films subsidiary. Another part, First Independent handles video retailing for the programmes.

Anchor man, if I may use that description, among the TV presenters is HTV's Bruce Hockin. Bruce is another who proves that professionals do stay here and use their skills to bring a smile to the news.

CHAPTER 31

FROME AT PLAY

— *Bob Beacham* —

There is excellent provision for people of Frome of all ages and abilities to play and keep fit, if such be their bent. All major games are catered for as well as a very wide range of minority sports and activities.

Frome Football Club has for many years sported a semi-professional team in the Western League, at Badgers Hill, where the 'Robins' once entertained Leyton Orient in the FA Cup. The Frome Sunday Football League runs to four divisions and forty-five teams, thus prising around five hundred local men from their beds for the 10.30 am kick-off. There is also a ladies team.

There is a very successful Rugby Club which fields four teams every Saturday. Sundays are mainly for the youngsters, who play in teams between the ages of seven and seventeen. This section is run almost entirely by parents. The Under-Seventeens played at Twickenham before an International crowd last season. The new Rugby Clubhouse at Gypsy Lane is the envy of many, with full banqueting facilities and a multi-gym and physiotherapy suite to boot. The Gypsy Lane Complex also offers four Football pitches, two Cricket and a grass Hockey pitch.

Karate kids.

The Summer Game prospers at Fromefield where Frome Cricket Club consistently figure in the top three of the Alliance League. The Ground figures in the record books as where Harold Gimblett of Somerset and England scored a sixty-three minute century on his County debut in 1935. The Club has provided three Frome men to the County game and one of them now coaches the juniors, who compete at four age levels. There are also numerous village teams.

The large sports complex now known as Frome Leisure Centre has a 25m indoor Swimming pool with teaching pool, a large Sports hall with marked games courts and a climbing wall, a games deck, indoor Bowls hall, Squash courts, solarium and a social lounge. They are proud of their state of the art twenty-seven station fitness room with qualified staff. There are floodlit outdoor pitches and there are plans for an international size all-weather Hockey pitch.

Even more Squash facilities exist at Frome Squash Club, and there is a smaller but very well resourced Sports hall available for public hire at the Frome Youth Club, where there are also plans for artificial floodlit Netball courts. Frome has a long history of Amateur Boxing and its club has provided a number of officials who have distinguished themselves in the National and International arenas. The club provides for schoolboys upwards.

Rugby is a major youth activity. Training starts at seven. Boys and girls are equals in this Under 13s league match.

For those attracted to more leisurely pursuits, there are Indoor and Outdoor Bowls Clubs, and numerous Skittles, Darts and Pool leagues. There is a thriving Angling Association and two Golf courses. Badminton, Trampolining, Chess, Judo, Dragon Boxing, Shotokan Karate, Tae Kwon-do, Basketball, Archery, Athletics, Canoeing, Cycling, Tennis, Caving, Rambling, Table Tennis, Sailing and Sub-Aqua are among many other local sports clubs. Being set in a large farming community, there are, of course many active Field Sports.

In spite of this marvellous wealth of sport, of all kinds, there is strong pressure for provision for more. This must be a healthy sign.

CHAPTER 32

ON THE
INTERNATIONAL SCENE

— Hilary Daniel —

Frome has long looked outward into the wider world. During the early decades of the 19th Century, when the town's cloth industry was in decline and unemployment was at a high level, there was a very substantial emigration to Upper Canada, as Ontario was then called, with assisted passages being provided by local philanthropists.

There was a further wave of emigration during the early 1900s, when a considerable number of young men went West to seek their fortunes, some of whom returned to Europe and to Frome with the Canadian forces during World War I, and some of whose sons did the same during World War II.

South Africa and Australia also beckoned, and Frome was remembered by her exiles in the naming of the small town of Frome near London in Ontario, and Lake Frome and the homestead of Frome Downs in South Australia.

One of the most celebrated early Australian links was with Mitraville, said to have been founded by a Frome man. In July 1911, the Premier of New South Wales, the Hon J S T McGowen, excited a great deal of public interest by visiting Frome to plant a Coronation oak tree in Victoria Park, and Frome and Mitraville exchanged flags.

Local archivist Hilda Massey, and historian Derek Gill, are kept busy putting overseas enquirers in touch with their roots in the Frome area.

Frome Rotary Club was early in making a twinning arrangement in 1963 with the newly formed Rotary Club de Bayeux, in Normandy. This link has prospered ever since, the clubs visiting each other in alternate years.

In 1975 Frome signed a formal twinning agreement with Chateau-Gontier in Mayenne, in France, a market town of some 13,000 inhabitants with a hilly mediaeval street pattern very reminiscent of Frome's. After the rather formal arrangements of the early days, many direct links have come to be forged between sporting, arts, musical and other groups, so that there is scarcely a month in the year when people from either town are not making some private arrangement to meet on one side of the Channel or the other to further their own special interests.

There are dozens of families who have developed deep friendships on a personal level, and important family events regularly involve invitations to weddings, anniversaries and so forth in the other country. Eventually Frome twinned with Chateau-Gontier's other twin, the German town of Murrhardt in Baden-Wurttemberg, a place of similar size in the fairy-tale surroundings of the Swabian forests.

Thus a tripling arrangement between the three towns was formed and this has also fostered, and the exchanges have grown to include the Town Band, Army Cadet Band, the Youth Orchestra and Youth Choir, the Chamber of Commerce, the Philatelists, the Fire Brigade, the Methodist Church, the Tennis Club, the Frome Singers, the Cycling Club, the Bounce Club, the Blood Donors and many others who have found firm friends with similar interests in all three countries.

Almost all the schools take part in exchanges, some very closely. A most imaginative local initiative has been the European Community of Stones, an

Town twinning signs, well kept and decorated with flowers, are prominent on major approaches to Frome.

open air theatre flanked by twelve large stones, one presented by each of the twelve nations of the European Community, brought over in 1992. At the opening of the Ecos Theatre, youth groups from Spain, Portugal and other countries further widened Frome's horizons. This was funded by Messrs Foster Yeoman, the major quarry group, and supported by the Town Council.

The pupils of Frome College have a long history of really ambitious exploratory adventure trips, from New Guinea to the Icelandic lava flows, and the wastes of the Sahara desert, and have been involved with Operation Raleigh. The Town Council backed support to a Romanian village near Cluj after the collapse of the Communist regime, and welcomed a party of young people from Russia.

The nearby village of Nunney has formed an association which brings over children affected by the Chernobyl disaster for a welcome and most generous annual holiday in the area.

All these activities have earned Frome the distinction of being the only town in Britain to have been awarded the Council of Europe's Diploma during 1995, the first step towards achieving the coveted Flag of Honour.

CHAPTER 33

FROME'S PLANS FOR THE FUTURE

— Andrew Prince —

At the beginning of the 18th century Frome had a population of close to 10,000 people. It was four times the size of Bath and was an important commercial centre built on the cloth trade.

During the 19th century as a result of the industrial revolution, Frome fell on hard times and the cloth trade moved north to the dark satanic mills of Lancashire. By 1960 the population of our town had only risen to just over 14,000 people.

During the 1970s and 80s the population of Frome started to rise dramatically. This was caused by both an increase in lifespan and a movement of people from the larger cities into the countryside and market towns.

In 1991 census figures show Frome now has a population of 23,159 of which 11,751 are in work or seeking work. What will happen to our population in the future? The Mendip economic profile suggests that by the year 2011 our population will have grown by a further 14.6% to 26,550 and our labour force will have increased by 14.2% to 13,450.

As a result of falling birth rate and an ageing population almost all of this growth in population will occur in the 45 plus age group with the majority in the 'baby boomer' 45–65 age grouping.

Over the next 20 years with a continually expanding population there will be pressure to provide additional housing and jobs for an increasingly ageing population. There will also be a need to provide adequate shopping and leisure facilities for a population with a growing amount of leisure time.

Looking at industry first of all, as without doubt this could have the largest impact on the supply of additional jobs, the simple solution is to attract a subsidiary of a major multi-national company which would set up on the edge of Frome and provide 1,000 new semi-skilled jobs.

There are a number of pitfalls to this solution, not least the difficulties of attracting and then keeping a business of that size.

The few businesses of this scale that are relocating, are going to development areas that provide grant aid, rate free periods and preferably easy access to the country's motorway network, Frome cannot offer this, although completion of Bath's bypass to the M4 will help considerably.

The solution is to encourage the growth of local businesses which as they develop will trade with other businesses. As already discussed in 'Commerce In Frome' the development of Mendip Foods and Hardings are both the most significant and most recent example of trend. Businesses of this type are more able to survive recessions and provide steady growth of employment opportunities.

It is important for the growth of these businesses that we provide adequately serviced industrial land. Currently at Wessex Fields, Frome has 2.7 hectares of serviced industrial land and it is hoped that in due course the Coalway Lane site covering 6 hectares on the north-east edge of Frome will be similarly serviced.

In 1991 Frome was the pilot for the Task Force concept, now being introduced in many towns across Somerset. The Task Force is a grouping of town, district and county councillors covering the Frome area together with representatives of other organisations such as the Police, Chamber of Commerce, Civic Society and education.

The Task Force is a consultative body which local government uses as a test bed for its ideas on developing our town. It also gives the local community an important opportunity to influence these proposals and also bring forward their own alternatives and ideas for local government to consider.

A recent example of this is the current introduction of a new and much clearer signposting of Frome. This was a Chamber of Commerce initiative presented to Task Force. Local government provided officer time to come up with recommendations which our local councils agreed to fund.

It is from the continued focusing of attention on Frome and the ideas that this generates that the Task Force can play such an important role in modelling the future of our community. The Task Force meets regularly and is open to the public. Time, date and venue of the next meeting can be obtained from either the Town Council or District Council offices.

The town centre of Frome has exercised many people's minds over the last decade and has created much heat and light, not however always in the same proportions. Our town centre showed rapid growth of services in the early 1970s with the opening of Westway Centre in 1973 and Kingsway Centre in 1974. There followed two decades of stagnation. No further new town centre development occurred and only one edge of town D.I.Y. store was opened in 1986.

In 1990 Frome Market relocated from its town centre site to Standerwick trebling in size overnight but leaving a large hole in the heart of Frome.

A number of proposals were considered culminating in a proposal for a new shopping centre anchored by a large supermarket. This proposal was effectively killed by the public enquiry in 1992 which decided to award planning permission for two edge of town sites at Wessex Fields and Wallbridge to Safeway and Sainsburys. This decision probably represented the low point in our town centre's fortunes.

Whilst the opening of Sainsburys undoubtedly reduced the number of people doing

International Business Systems: a modern conference centre.

*Blue House. This fine almshouse of the 1720s has
bathrooms of the 1990s.*

their food shopping in Trowbridge, it also sucked
business from the town centre leading to the closure
of some businesses particularly in the weaker areas
such as Catherine Hill and Badcox.

There is no point in complaining about edge of
town shopping despite a recent change of policy by
the government. It's here and it's successful.

There is no doubt that the combination of clean
environment with free convenient parking offered by
Sainsburys is what our shoppers would want in our
town centre. The plans now being put in place are
designed to raise the standards, ease of access and
provision of shops in the town centre to that level.

At the moment only 55% of our community
regularly shops in Frome – that figure should be 90%.

The Donaldsons' report in 1993 showed that the
major concerns were with the provision of an adequate
choice of stores, particularly larger multiples and with
adequate provision of free short term parking. The latter
particularly influenced by the West Wiltshire towns.

The Health Centre next to Frome's Hospital.

A rare exception from the brutal sixties: timeless Frome Tool & Gauge.

What could we do to counter this continuing flow of bad news about our town centre? How do we attract our shoppers back to Frome's historic centre?

This is where the good news begins.

The relocation of Frome Market released 3.5 acres of development land in the Market Yard. More recently it has become clear that Singers would be prepared to relocate to an edge of town site which, if these negotiations prove successful, will lead to the release of a further 11 acres of development land adjoining the Market Yard site.

This would be the largest parcel of town centre land available for development in the West Country.

After the collapse of the Raglan scheme as a result of Sainsburys' decision, Mendip District Council put the Market Yard scheme out to tender.

The winning scheme produced by Bartlett Construction envisages an 18,000 sq.ft. anchor foodstore and a number of non-food retail shops in the 4,000 to 6,000 sq.ft. size that multiple retailers demand and Frome currently lacks. The scheme will be built in a neo-Georgian style. This scheme, smaller than the Raglan plans, takes into account the ability of the town's roads to take the extra traffic without the need for a costly road improvement scheme.

An important first phase of the scheme, completed Autumn 1995, is the £1 million refurbishment of the Westway Precinct. This has removed the starkness of the 1960s design, replacing it with a Georgian style more in keeping with the historic centre of the town.

The centre now incorporates a considerably extended Martins as well as a number of other enlarged shops. Phase Two, the Market Yard development is now proposed to start in 1997.

The scheme will have a 550 space car park which the developer insists will have a period of free parking. It is worth at this point just looking at the arguments for two hours free parking.

Currently with the start of the free parking scheme in Shepton Mallet every publicly owned car parking space within 15 miles of Frome is free at the point of use for at least two hours. Donaldsons' report showed that 50% of the people in Frome, which is the Mendip town most exposed to the effects of West Wilts free parking policy, felt the cost of parking was a significant reason for not shopping in town.

The district is currently undertaking a trial in Frome to measure the effect of free parking on the local retail economy. Hopefully by the time this article is read Frome will have a free parking scheme.

It has always been understood that a period of free parking is not a solution in its own right to Frome's retailing problems. It is however an important building brick in the revival of our town centre.

It is important with the developments affecting the Westway/Market Yard/Singers area that we do not move the focus of the town completely to that area. There are a number of initiatives underway to ensure that the other areas of the town centre are strengthened and regenerated. Scott Road is being re-surfaced and 'enhanced'. This is being completed by the end of 1995.

In 1996 engineering evaluation work is to be undertaken to see if it is feasible to narrow

Artist's impression of the new Westway Centre.

the carriageway width in the Market Place to 7 metres. This combined with additional 'humped' pedestrian crossings is designed to make the Market Place less of a barrier to pedestrians crossing between the two halves of the town centre.

There are longer term plans to make King Street, Church Street and Eagle Lane access only to traffic. Plans have also been discussed to completely pedestrianise the Market Place. However existing roads cannot take the capacity of traffic that currently passes through our town centre – some 19,000 vehicles each day.

Artist's impression of how Library Square could look.

There are thoughts of an inner relief road system, although no final route plans and funding have as yet been agreed, or are likely to be in the forseeable future.

This may however not be totally bad news as one criticism aimed at Trowbridge is that it is now submerged by a sea of relief roads which have totally destroyed the character of the town.

The piece by piece approach now being undertaken in Frome will hopefully ensure that the historic centre of the town is retained and improved.

Frome with over 500 listed groups of buildings, many of them dating from the 16th century has more listed buildings than the rest of the Mendip District combined and was described in the recent Civic Trust report as having a unique town centre of national importance.

In any programme for the revival of a town centre it is important that there is someone in overall control so that redevelopment does not end up in a piecemeal and uncoordinated shambles. In early 1994 a town centre manager was appointed to oversee the regeneration of Frome town centre by Mendip District Council. Frome is one of the smallest towns by population to have a town centre manager.

One of the first responsibilities of our manager has been to regenerate Catherine Hill an area that has been particularly hard hit in recent years.

Crime or possibly the fear of crime has increasingly become an issue in our town, as elsewhere.

As a result of co-funding by our County and District councils a trial camera monitoring scheme became operational in the Westway/Market Yard car park area early in 1995. The full first phase of the scheme which will cover the Market Place is due to become operational by the end of 1995. There has already been a recordable drop in incidents of crime within the trial camera area.

In conclusion, I would use the analogy of comparing Frome to a great ship slowing down. Over a number of years in the late 1980s and early 1990s the town lost direction. We lost jobs and more importantly our way. I believe in the last four years with the commitment of councillors and community alike many decisions have been taken that will lead to a revitalisation of the economic heart of our community. The ship is beginning almost imperceptibly to gather speed again.

I believe that by the year 2000 we will be able to see a very changed town but one that is vital, active and prosperous, a Frome to be proud of.

POSTSCRIPT

— Editor —

I hope any stranger to Frome, having read this book, will agree with us that Frome is a special town. Not only its many attractive buildings and interesting streets, but the imaginative and determined nature of so many of its citizens to get things going, whether they be born locally or have made their homes here.

I have been pleased to learn a lot more about Frome and its people, in compiling this book. Plans for the rejuvenation of locally run-down areas are here to read about, and many changes will already be evident before this book leaves the press. These plans have taken a long time to bear fruit, and were delayed and much modified because of the deep recession which brought disaster to so many other towns' promising new developments. They will no doubt be subject to Frome's usual robust comments, but it is difficult to imagine that the town will not benefit considerably from them. I hope that this book will have disseminated some of the good news which seems to travel with so much more difficulty than the bad news.

We are confident that the bottoming out of the recession and the excellent plans for redevelopment mean that this beautiful town with its resourceful people is at the beginning of a recovery with an improvement of the town's fabric and employment prospects, giving a better chance to its young people, at last.

If the Rotary Club of Frome's initiative in commissioning this book, and the inspiration and generosity of all its contributors, can act as a catalyst in the process of this recovery, then its purpose will have been realised. Can I take this space to give sincere thanks to all the marvellous authors, from many walks of life, including quite a few professional writers. Andrew Prince wrote his two excellent articles on top of a frantic work schedule but has also been a great encouragement by his unwavering enthusiasm and pragmatism. In spite of the cynicism, apathy, conservatism and lethargy he must have met, he has remained amongst the enthusiasts, long may he remain so. I am grateful for his helpful suggestions and for personally recruiting help when needed.

Right: An arc of Ecos stones form European backcloth to youthful performers: symbol of the future.

Not a single person turned me down and all generously allowed me to modify their writing, where necessary, to fit in with the style of the book, to reduce duplication, and to keep the book to the intended length. My thanks to our wonderful photographers whose work so enlivens the book.

Our prestigious and busy printers have been extremely generous in making no charge for all their work, and their staff have been helpful and patient; a special thanks to Steve Opie who has shown a special interest in guiding the book through all stages of printing. Our paper suppliers have been most generous to donate the paper in these times of fast rising costs. A special thank you to Glyn Martin for allowing us to use his beautiful water colour on the cover. Les White gave me help and encouragement at just the right time and Alan Sandall's special knowledge and hard work when he is so busy in his Rotary Presidential year has been invaluable.

Copies of this book will be sent to a number of people whose interest might benefit the town and to members of the media. Any profits after considerable post and packaging charges and other costs will go to the Frome Rotary Club's Account for community work within the town.

Frome has a great future as it has had a great past. Pessimists can never be converted to optimists, because such is their nature; but people who are neither are more likely to feel good about things, if, being better informed about Frome's remarkable progress and future plans, their conversation includes good news as well as bad. People who feel good, undoubtedly perform better and have better ideas, whilst grasping any help which is available from outside, it is from the genius of its people Frome's future prosperity will come.

Butler & Tanner's main buildings. Aerial photography by Commission-Air Peterborough.

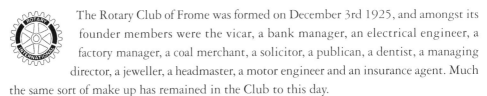 The Rotary Club of Frome was formed on December 3rd 1925, and amongst its founder members were the vicar, a bank manager, an electrical engineer, a factory manager, a coal merchant, a solicitor, a publican, a dentist, a managing director, a jeweller, a headmaster, a motor engineer and an insurance agent. Much the same sort of make up has remained in the Club to this day.

What is Rotary? Briefly it is a world fellowship of business and professional men and women, united in the ideal of service. It has more than 27,000 clubs with a membership of well over one million, in more than 152 countries. The spirit and ideal of Rotary which has attracted so many men and women of different races, faiths and cultures is to encourage the development of acquaintances as an opportunity for service. It encourages high ethical standards in business and community life, and the advancement of international understanding, goodwill and peace.

Our Club has been glad to support the local community and overseas communities in need, for seventy years and hopes to continue to do so for the next seventy years and more.

Further Reading

'*The Book of Frome*', '*Frome through the ages*', '*Frome place names*', '*Frome in picture postcards*' 3 volumes, '*Crime and Punishment in Regency Frome*' all by Michael McGarvie. '*The making of Frome*' by Peter Belham. '*Frome then and now*' by G Russell. '*Frome in old photographs*' by Derek Gill. '*Bath Street, Frome*' by Derek Gill. '*The Buildings of Frome*' by Rodney Goodall. '*Going, Going, Gone! History of Frome's Livestock Market*' by Alan Sandall.